ABOUT

Ram Gidoomal, a Fellow of the Royal Society of Arts is a successful businessman of East African Asian origin. After having earned his Bachelor's degree in Physics from the prestigious Imperial College of Science and Technology in London, after a brief spell of postgraduate studies, he joined Lloyds Bank International Corporate Finance services, before going on to head a large Geneva based multinational. He decided to quit the world of active business at the age of 40 to pursue actively his interests in charities. He has been successful in raising large amounts of moneys for various causes for the suffering people of the world. In addition to his activities in charities, of which he is one of the founders of South Asian Concerns and Chairman of Christmas Crackers Trust, Ram is also an advisor to the Prince's Youth Business Trust and a director of the South London Training and Enterprise Council. Ram has authored three books, including the current Karma 'n' Chips and is currently working on other titles, all of which try to examine the practice and meaning of modern day spirituality as a result of new economic and spiritual environmental factors. Ram has also been a Cambridge University examiner on Hinduism.

Mike Fearon is a professional writer and journalist, broadcaster and speaker who has contributed articles to a number of newspaper and periodicals, among them *The Independent, Church Times* and *Record Collector*. He has been the editor of *New Consciousness*. He has had published seven books, and this book is the second that he has co-authored with Ram. He is currently working with Ram on a sequel to this book.

Unless otherwise indicated, biblical quotations are from the
New International Version © 1973, 1978, 1984 by the
International Bible Society.

Produced in England
Typesetting and Graphic Arts by PM Graphics
Cover Design by Sheena Clarke and PM Graphics
Printed in Denmark at Norhaven.

WPC is an imprint of Wimbledon Publishing Company
29 Hartfield Road, London SW19 3SG. Tel: 081 544 9901

KARMA 'n' CHIPS

Dedicated to
Phillipe and Wendy Berthoud

In loving memory of their sincere love and friendship.

The sun will no more be your light by day,
nor will the brightness of the moon shine on you,
for the Lord will be your everlasting light,
and your God will be your Glory.

ISIAH 60: 19

KARMA 'n' CHIPS

Ram Gidoomal
and
Mike Fearon

WIMBLEDON PUBLISHING COMPANY

ACKNOWLEDGEMENTS

Many people have helped in the preparation of this book. I would particularly like to thank Dr Raju Abraham, Prabhu Guptara, Ms Judith Parker, Sunil Raheja, Basil Scott and Robin Thompson for painstakingly proof reading the manuscript and their helpful feedback and comments.

My wife Sunita and my children Ravi, Nina and Ricki for all their support and encouragement (and patience!).

CONTENTS

FOREWORD

By Professor Prabhu Guptara

The famous Indian mystic, Sadhu Sundar Singh, once told the story of a man who, on a walk in the mountains, sat down for a bit of rest. He had used a piece of bamboo as a sort of walking stick and chancing to hit a nearby rock with the bamboo, was intrigued by the hollow sound which came, as though, from the rock.

Then he realised with a start that it was not the rock which was hollow, but the bamboo in his hand.

Too often, we think that a particular philosophy or opinion or novel or work of art is hollow, when it is in fact our approach which is hollow.

Of course, the opposite can also be the case: we can think that something is quite solid but, when we really investigate it, we may discover that it is not as solid as we thought.

Karma 'n' Chips is bold and innovative, and dares to ask incredibly difficult questions: Are our traditional Hindu ways really as solid as we think? Is Christianity quite as solid as Indian and Western Christians seem to think?. Or are both hollow?

Can the mysteries of life be understood to any degree? Do traditional religions throw any real light which a modern thinking person can understand and accept?

Even trained philosophers and accomplished mystics have found such issues difficult. I will not pretend that authors have made the issues easy to understand. I do not think that any one can make these matters easy. But they have attempted to tackle these things in a way that is open and jargon-free as possible.

That is one reason why I appreciate and recommend this book.

I must say, however, that there are many things about which Ram and I disagree. Our understanding of Hindu ideas and beliefs is different, indeed sometimes radically different - though that is due as much to the variety and contradictions of our own traditions themselves as it is to the difference between Ram's perspective and mine.

Our understanding of Christianity too is naturally different - though we are relatively close in our respective understandings of Christ the Lord. Like most Indians, I feel instinctively attracted to the beauty, simplicity and moral power of Christ's extraordinary personality, in the light of whose presence most of our so-called present-day gurus can be seen to be both limited and imperfect.

But if the book's position contrasts so strongly with mine in several areas, why do I so willingly write a Foreward?

First, because Ram is one of the most honest and open people I know. For that reason, I consider seriously everything he says.

Second, because Ram is a highly creative person. He brings his demonstrated entrepreneurship in the commercial world of business, in the practical challenge of raising funds for charity, now, to the rather more airy-fairy world of ideas and philosophy. His scholarship can be argued about, and no doubt will be argued about, principally because he refuses to approach the subject only through the highways approved and controlled by Western scholarship. Sadly, even Indian scholars have ususally allowed their views to be constrained by Western views of Indian religions and spiritualities. Well, Ram certainly does not do homage to Western scholars - or to Indian scholars for that matter. Though he is acquainted with an astonishingly wide variety of their views.

The authors are vigorous and clear in their analysis, presenting it is as simple and understandable a way as possible, keeping a continuous thread through the various religious and philosophical positions they examine on each of the issues discussed.

One great curse of Indian traditional attitudes is that, under the guise of religious and philosophical liberalism, there is intellectual fascism; in the quest for spiritual liberty, you are not supposed to ask questions or think for yourself; you are allowed to believe only what some guru or "master" teaches.

Ram is undoubtedly a guru, but his kind off guruship refuses to close minds. Ram is interested in opening minds as well as hearts and spirits.

Sadhu Sundar Singh also told the story of a beggar who, all his life, sat near the central bus station in a big town in the Punjab and begged alms of passers by. When he died no one knew whether he was a Hindu, Muslim or Sikh, and so neither the Hindu communities, nor the Muslim and Sikh communities, wanted to take on the financial and organisational burden of the funeral rites. So it was decided to bury the body at the very spot where he used to beg and where he died - that was, simply, the cheapest and the easiest thing to do. And it was somehow appropriate, wasn't it, for him to be buried at the same place where he used to beg.

Well, they started digging the grave. And discovered to their utter amazement that, under the very spot where he used to beg, there was an ancient treasure.

The man had lived and died penniless - and all the time he had been sitting on top of a untold riches.

Karma 'n' Chips is for the readers who believe that there is indeed a real treasure to be found, spiritually - but who may have no idea of how to go about the process of locating the treasure.

This book offers a stimulating exploration of the area. And the demanding work of climbing the mountains or trudging through the long flat spells is made lighter, as far as possible, by Mike's gentle humour and the twinkle in Ram's eye.

If I recollect correctly, Jesus the Lord once said that the door is opened to the person who knocks. People who seek with all their heart do find. That, according to Jesus the Lord, is the only karma required to find the Truth. And without that karma, he said, we will all have had our chips; without that karma, nothing counts.

Read this book, then, with a passionate hunger for truth. Be deeply open to all the questions the book raises. You will find, as I did, that even if you disagree with some of what is said, the process of understanding and working your way through *Karma 'n' Chips* can help you understand both karma and chips. This book will help you to distinguish solidity from hollwoness. It can therefore bring you closer to the Truth. If you are willing to do your part. That is, if you are willing to search with your mind and spirit as well as your heart.

Publisher's Note: Professor Prabhu Guptara is widely known as a writer, lecturer and broadcaster and is the oldest-established British consultant in the fields of Organisation Transformation and of Globalisation. He is the author of several books, among them Indian Spirituality. He is also included in DEBRETT'S *Peoples of Today*.

PROLOGUE

It may come as a surprise to those who consider Hinduism to be the oldest religion in the world, to discover that the word 'Hinduism' actually has its origins early in the colonial period, and is only about 200 years old!

Colonialist dubbed everyone who lived around the Indus river 'Hindus' (usually spelt 'hindoos' at that time). Rather than make any serious attempt to understand the inter-related family of religions being practiced by these South Asians, it was easier to lump them all together and call the whole lot 'Hinduism'.

This cack-handed approach to non-European religions eloquently typifies the piecemeal approach to Asian spirituality and religious traditions with which east-west relations began and have continued. Though the Gita first appeared in English nearly 200 years ago, patronisingly called the 'Bible of the East', it was nearly a hundred years later before translations of the Upanishads and other key texts began to appear in western languages.

'Hinduism can hardly be called a religion,' writes Raimundo Panikkar. 'It is rather a bundle of religious traditions. We should readily understand the instinctive reaction of the people of India against being levelled down to a single "Hinduism". Strictly speaking, Hinduism does not exist.' Hindus, of course, much prefer the term *sanatana dharma* - the eternal law - as the title for this family of religious traditions, of which tribal religions are really too far removed to be considered a part.

Our earlier book **Sari 'n' Chips** explored the culture clashes experienced by Asians living outside the homeland. **Karma 'n' Chips** does the same from the standpoint of religious and ideological conflicts. This is not simply an academic exercise. Religious discrimination is perhaps the cruelest prejudice of all - a frequent source of anguish and family turmoil. What is a good Hindu parent to do if the son seems interested in some strange religion that seems very different from the family's traditional religious faith? How can disaster and family scandal be averted?

One young man broke away from the religious traditions of his parents at the age of fifteen. 'When I told my mother what I had done, she became very angry. She told my father, and they both pressured me to leave the family home. I had nowhere to go, no alternative shelter, so I was very fortunate that my parents didn't simply turn me onto the streets. They stopped feeding me though, and I used to cry under my bedsheets at night.'

It's not just Hindu families that have the problem. A convert from Islam was driven out of his home village. No one would so much as inform him of his father's death. When he went back to the village later in life, no one would welcome him, or offer shelter. They believed his actions meant a betrayal of the family, with a snide insinuation that they were all wrong in their beliefs; even though this was not his intention. It is sad when one side accuses the other of religious intolerance, if neither side is prepared to see the other's viewpoint.

On a BBC *Kilroy* programme in which Ram Gidoomal appeared, a western convert explained that - though she hadn't actually been thrown out of the house - tensions were so pronounced that her brother wouldn't even drink tea from the same teapot from which she had poured a cup! Often it is the sheer triteness and appalling arrogance of religious prejudice and persecution that is the hardest to bear.

Bernard Levin has written in *The Times*: 'There are different kinds of savages. Perhaps the worst of them are those believe - or, rather, claim to believe - that they have been given some kind of message from their deity which permits them - indeed orders them - to demand that those professing a different faith must renounce it, on pain of ostracism, expulsion, imprisonment or ultimately execution.' *(18th Jan 1994)*

Tens of thousands of Asian familes are facing the same problem, all across the globe.

Many household heads cannot comprehend that a family member might want so deeply to explore their personal beliefs that they might decided to follow a different religion from the faith they learned at their mother's knee. 'How can you change the religion you were born into?' they cry anxiously, often feeling that they have somehow failed. But there need be no condemnation involved; the western approach to religion is that *each individual has the right to make a personal choice about the faith that he or she will follow* - or even to have no faith at all. It's as natural as the cold climate and the rotten weather!

Devotion to God is surely an excellent practice, to be warmly commended both by families in India and in the west. But to accept what appear to be the religious values and traditions of the host country seems like a brutal denial of a person's Asian roots. Often expatriate families feel that they are still 'Indians', 'Pakistanis' or whatever, even when they have renounced their citizenship and taken on a different nationality. Accepting that a valued family member can change their religion in the same way as they have changed their nationality is a harder task - *but it needn't be.*

When independence was first mooted in India early this century, many primitive tribes whose faith had little to do with orthodox religion suddenly found themselves designated as Hindus - without a 'by-your-leave' - because it was *politically expedient* to increase the number of 'Hindus' within the proposed borders of the Indian homeland. In *The Confusion Called Conversion*, author Sunder Raj estimates that tens of millions of non-Hindus have found themselves 'converted to Hinduism' by this sleight of hand. During the first quarter of the twentieth century alone, 'well over two crore of the tribals were "converted" by the Census enumerator to the Brahminical faith, ' says Sunder Raj. 'The tribal, however, still does not know that he has been "converted"...' (A crore is 10,000,000)

'Ah, but a change of faith is a shameful betrayal of the South Asian tradition,' says the anguished parent - wrongly. Sunder Raj shows that there is no one culture which can be called 'The South Asian Culture', any more than there is one fixed set of beliefs that can blithely be called Hinduism. India has four distinct racial cultures (Aryan, Dravidic, Mongoloid and Shudras) on which stand forty seperate major cultures and at least 1,200 sub-cultures. When an Asian is accused of betraying his culture, what exactly is meant by 'his culture?'

'My family tradition is one of being a tribe of head hunters,' laughs one convert. 'Does that mean that I should be a head hunter, too?'

The consequences of families adopting an unreasonable and unfeeling attitude to members who explore other religious avenues and options can be dire. Pushed too far, valued family members can be driven prematurely to cut themselves off from the protection of the family unit, running needless risks all because of simple misunderstandings. The overwhelming pressures on Asians caught in unsurmountable family conflicts has led many down the dark alleyways of despair and driven them to take their own lives.

Yet the main root cause of religious tensions is frequently nothing more than misapprehension, misunderstanding, and lack of familiarity with the other spiritual views that are prevalent in the pluralist society that has engulfed the whole globe.

The day has passed when each religion could be neatly

compartmentalised and followed unquestioningly by whole nations and continents. Spiritual fulfillment is increasingly an individual quest which each of us must attend to for him or herself. How can we blame or condemn others when they find inner peace and fulfillment of a manner that we do not yet know ourselves? Are we so weak and insecure that we persecute our own colleagues and family members simply because they wish to follow a slightly different spiritual path from our own?

Let us all have the courage and compassion to accept in others a solid religious faith that perhaps we have yet to discover for ourselves. Instead of criticising and comdemning, let us be open enough to understand the devoutly held religious views of other traditions - and perhaps to reconsider the religion that we profess for ourselves. Open enquiry must surely be a more beneficial answer to the problem of disagreement over religious matters than the petty jealousies and bickerings that so ill befit those who claim to be following an ancient and honourable spiritual path.

Though this book was originally intended to address the problems faced by Asians in the west, we are fully aware that it may also serve more general needs in homes and schools, colleges and clinics, workplaces and places of worship. It is our wish that Asians and Westerners alike might learn more of each other's vital religious traditions - and perhaps to come to a far deeper understanding of their own spirituality - through reading the pages that follow.

Karma 'n' Chips is not a book you can just 'dip into'. Though presented in the plainest possible terms, the ideas develop logically from one another, and are of an intricacy that mean the book is best read systematically, a chapter or two at a time. Chapters three and four, in particular, require close study if their concepts are to be fully understood.

A new age is dawning. It's time to move out of the darkness and into the light.

Mike Fearon and Ram Gidoomal.

London. May 1994.

INTRODUCTION

No one who was there would ever forget the spectacle! At Ayodhya, in Northern India, on December 6th 1992, the three beautiful domes of an ancient mosque were razed to the ground in a plume of dust under the blows of 4,000 Hindu fundamentalists. Beneath a blood-red sun, these reckless *kar sevaks*, or holy warriors, were spurred on by tens of thousands of vehement supporters lining nearby ridges, urging death and destruction. Five of the *kar sevaks* who hadn't moved quickly enough when the domes came down were crushed beneath the debris.

The blast of conch shells blended with the throbbing drum beats; crashing cymbals and eerie chanting filled the smoky air as the 464 year old Babri mosque was utterly demolished and the remains carted away as trophies by lines of volunteers.

Young *kar sevaks* leapt about shouting *'Jai Shri Ram!'* meaning 'Hail Lord Rama'. They set fire to the vehicles used as roadblocks to keep out the police. As the flames and the black smoke rose higher, security forces arrived wielding batons and employing tear gas to drive back the holy warriors - now a mob fully 300,000 strong - who had 'liberated' the Muslim shrine in the belief that it covered the birthplace of the Hindu god Rama...

The desecrated - and desolated - site was secured and ringed with razor wire guarded by paramilitary commandos, but the repercussions began to reverberate around India, and across the world. Rioting in a thousand villages and a dozen major cities across the country left 1,100 dead and 4,000 wounded; in Bombay, forty-eight buses were damaged and ten places of worship attacked by mobs up to 10,000 strong; 3,000 arrests were made; five religious organisations were banned by the government; and the leaders of a major opposition party taken into custody. Not since the convulsions of partitioning had India known such bloodshed.

Asian communities in Britain soon felt the tit-for-tat reprisals. The Shree Krishna temple in West Bromwich was torched in an act described by the press as 'sheer barbarism'. Hindu property in Coventry, Birmingham, Bradford and Derby was also attacked in the Islamic backlash. In the free for all, a mosque in Forest Gate and a Sikh temple in Luton came under attack; two petrol bombs were thrown at the Krishna temple in Bolton - while it was filled with worshippers - though fortunately no one was hurt.

In Bangladesh, many Hindu temples were attacked, and three Asian children died when their home was set afire by religious extremists. Months later, many Christians in India were still expressing their terror of militant Hinduism, fearing that it would soon be their own churches which were purged.

'It is a violation of Hinduism,' a professor at New Delhi's Jawaharlal Nehru University told *Time* magazine. 'It has never been a crusading religion like Christianity or Islam; but now that perception of tolerance has been shattered.'

Religion holds powerful forces at its command which, once released unchecked, can turn the clock back to dark ages once believed to have long since passed. Holy wars loom large in the annals of human history, and if this book can play a part in reducing the religious frictions and ugly tensions which lead to such outbreaks of violence, it will have been worth writing.

Religion can also be a pacifying influence, joining disparate families together in social, cultural and spiritual harmony. In *The Miracle that is Hindu Dharma,* Ram Chandra Gupta writes: 'Religion provides us with an appropriate means to probe into the reality that is not in the outside world, but within ourselves. It is a matter of experience. It is not an awakening from a swoon, but a transformation of one's being.'

Religion is often misinterpreted and misunderstood. Minor disagreements can escalate out of all proportion if neither side is really aware of the origins and development of its own beliefs. Often, bizarre practises and beliefs which have no part in a religion's original formulation can be the spark that ignites an inferno. Only by learning what a religion *really* teaches, once all the cultural accretions and historical baggage has been stripped away, can we know a faith's spiritual heartland - truth that is worth defending at all costs - and detect non-essentials that are better dispensed with lest they lead to unnecessary bloodletting.

Spirituality certainly cannot be ignored. Ever since people first looked up into the starry sky and felt very small, they have sought answers to the 'big' questions - *Why am I here? What is the purpose of living?* Religions have sought to provide the solutions. All the major world faiths have their geographical origins in either the Middle East or South Asia. Hindu, Buddhist, Jewish, Christian and Muslim belief all originated in Asia. The spirituality that stemmed from that relatively small proportion of the earth's surface has embraced the globe.

Each of these faiths has given rise to countless volumes of sacred writings, commentaries and explanations; but this book will concentrate mainly on Hindu theory and practice, and in its relation to those other faiths.

An Overview

Hindu thought attempts to reconcile God and the world - without compromising God. In doing so, it frequently becomes so esoteric as to be almost incomprehensible to the layman. A Hindu priest of the Brahmin caste is needed to explain and intercede. Christianity had declined into a similar elitist phase by the fifteenth century, but has since become more accessible as it has discovered its original message from the Bible about the teaching and practice of Jesus. Many feel that Hinduism needs to be similarly accessible if it is to be fully understood by the masses.

Every believer sees his own tradition from the inside, so that for the believer it becomes a symbol of all that is true. **Karma'n'Chips** seeks to discover the insider's view, and to present it in a gently critical way, without condescension.

Living religions change - often through contact with other faiths. We will therefore occasionally contrast Hindu belief with Buddhist, Jain, Sikh, Jewish, Muslim and - particularly, since it is the dominant faith in the West - Christian beliefs. (A minority of Hindus are alarmed by Christianity, though we hope that this book will dismiss much of this groundless apprehension.) Common themes will be explored - revealing startling similarities and contrasting essential differences - to see whether there are aspects in each faith which can illuminate the others.

As this is primarily an exploration of Hindu belief and practice, albeit in a western context, we will take twelve key Hindu themes, and assimilate them with similar themes from other faiths (but mainly from the teachings of Jesus) to see the precise points at which divergence takes place if at all, and to examine the *reason* for the divergence. We will endeavour to explore Hindu thought and practice *within the context of its own background, seen through the eyes of its own philosophers and sages*.

We recognise that doctrine is only a picture or a model and not the reality itself. Religions meet in the heart, not in the mind. *We will not be comparing doctrines, but examining the essential truths which the doctrines seek to explain*.

There are three pressing cultural forces currently at play on

Asian spirituality in the west. Living in Britain, or any other western country, removes Hindu beliefs from much of the traditional context, and exposes people to the winds of other traditions; the west has a vibrant religious tradition of its own in Christianity; and the modern world is pluralist, with no one faith able to make claims to have a monopoly on the truth - at least, not without flak from other belief systems.

Hindus find that their beliefs are being modified - as they have been throughout most of history. Indeed many commonly accepted aspects of the faith are comparatively recent appendages! It is illogical for Hindus, then, to regard faiths like Christianity as 'younger upstarts' if they adhere to more recent additions, such as *Advaita Vedanta*.

Hindus generally do not loathe Christianity. Indeed, they are usually happy to make room for Christian beliefs within Hinduism's own astonishingly multi-faceted structure. A typical (though not universal) Hindu trait is to regard those of other faiths as being on different paths to the same ultimate destination. Other faiths are like other castes, with their own *dharmas*, within the great and mysterious scenario of sublime cosmic order. (We will cover the meaning of *dharma* in the first chapter.)

'Present day Hindus are in general convinced that all religions are good in as far as they lead men to perfection,' believes Panikkar. 'They would be inclined to accept and even join in with it, if Christianity would consent to give up its exclusiveness and its consequent claim to be the definitive religion.'

Many Hindus find it hurtful that Christians will not accept that there may be different ways to reach their sublime and mysterious God. Christians may be similarly offended by Hindus who expect them to sacrifice their distinctiveness, to become merged into some chaotic amalgamation of conflicting dogmas!

As Panikkar puts it: 'The deep-thinking Christian declines to judge Hinduism. God alone judges, through Christ. So long as men are pilgrims on earth, Christianity has not the right to separate the wheat from the chaff. Rather, in accepting Hinduism as it is, the Christian will find Christ already there.' That's quite a claim, and one which we will cover in the middle part of **Karma 'n' Chips**.

History

Because readers will be approaching this book from different levels of understanding, it is first necessary to provide a 'crash course' giving a basic historical perspective, and a rudimentary summary of the relevant religious texts of the adroit South Asian people. (Those who know their Vedas from their elbow, and who already have an understanding of the key points of Asian history, may like to proceed to the first chapter, and omit the brief primer which follows:)

'The exact idea of Hinduism is hard to define since the beliefs and practices of Hinduism differ greatly from one period of history to another, and within a given period of history from one region to another, and within a given region, from one class to another,' Dhavamony warns in his book *Classical Hinduism*.

The chief divisions in the historical development of Hinduism are: Vedism, Brahmanism, Classical period, Sectarian development, Medieval period, Modern Hinduism and Contemporary period, though none exist in 'watertight compartments'. The divisions merge with one another, disallowing clear demarcation.

As we will see, the weakness as well as the strength of the faith has always been the assimilation rather than the exclusion of other religious currents washing around it. Judaism, Jainism, Buddhism, Christianity and Islam have all contributed, though sometimes not in a way which an orthodox believer of one of those faiths would recognise!

The original faith of India is now lost in the mists of antiquity. A civilisation existed on the sub-continent four thousand years ago, but this original Harappan culture has left behind no clues to its nature other than a few fragments of broken pottery, skeletons lying in ruined cities, and a script that could not till recently be deciphered. For whatever reason, the civilisation entered a dark age which made it easy prey for the invading Aryans who arrived via what is now modern Iran around 1750 BC (Asian civilisations are notoriously difficult to date accurately).

The Aryans were nomadic cattle herders who brought with them, probably in waves over several hundred years, a new religion which perhaps fused with elements of an original Harappan faith. In oral form, they fetched thousands of sublime religious poems, which took written shape around 800BC - give or take about 300 years!

The oldest written collection is the *Rig Veda*, comprising 1,017 sanskrit hymns to a host of gods. The other three Vedas are the *Yajur Veda* (sacrificial formulae) the *Sama Veda* (melodies for chanting the hymns), and the *Atharva Veda* (spells and charms). The Vedas are augmented with the *Brahmanas*, texts written by and for Aryan priests to explain the perplexing sacrificial rituals around which the Vedic religion of that time revolved.

Gradually, priests of the *brahmin* caste began to gain more and more power as their rituals became increasingly elaborate. They began to see their role as *controlling*, rather than placating the mysterious gods to whom they sacrificed, and the faith moved into its Brahminist period. In reaction, theologians began a philosophical exploration of their beliefs, concerning God, humanity, the purpose of existence, and the mystery of what lies beyond the grave. These treatises were the *Upanishads*, written approximately 800-500BC. Of the 108 that have survived about a dozen are important. Exploration of the teachings of the Upanishads, from the universal to the deeply personal, makes up much of this book!

The advent of Buddhism and Jainism, circa 500BC, corresponded with decline in the sacrificial system, and an interchange of ideas with these new religions which led to a growth of philosophy amongst Hindus. Five centuries later, Christianity also unwittingly contributed to the mix, with its emphasis on devotion to the Supreme being. Classical Hindu belief emerged, offering three ways of growing close to God: *Karma yoga* (a variation on the old sacrificial system) *Jnana Yoga* (the way of knowledge, where common ground with Buddhism is particularly evident) and *Bhakti Yoga* (the way of devotion, borrowing from Christianity.)

At the same time as these strands of thought were being crystalised, two epic poems similarly took shape, the *Ramayana* and the *Mahabharata*, both set in India's mythical past. A part of the latter text, the *Bhagavad Gita*, is the primary text of the Bhakti school, though it is of late origin and not technically a part of the Hindu scriptures at all.

'Hindu culture has gone through a process of gradual degeneration and decay over the past seven or eight centuries,' says Pratima Bowes. She attributes this decay to the failure of Hindus to defend themselves from Islamic aggression in previous centuries, the caste system, and general decadence. The situation had become so bad by the nineteenth century that it was largely the work of European orientalists to make the Hindu scriptures generally available to Hindus themselves!

Hindu belief and practice today is a very different species from the original faith, as it developed from a blending of traditions over many centuries - a process that needs to occur again in our own age if the overall decay of Asian culture is to be halted, Bowes believes.

Karma 'n' Chips examines the liberating innovations that are being made to age-old devotional practices swept far from their cultural roots by waves of Asian immigrants. Paradoxically, the secret to the transformation of the moribund Asian faith and culture may lie in the west, where many dissenting voices claim that all organised religions have drawn a dark curtain across the blinding face of God. In a changing world, there are always free-spirited people dissatisfied with the old elitist ways, who are keen to tear down the curtain and bask in the glow of divinity unfettered by the restrictive religious past...

Sacred Texts

Overall, it's worth pointing out to the non-Asian reader that the types of Hindu scriptures differ from one another in the same way that, say, in the Bible the epistles, the wisdom books, the historic books and the law books are different in style. The Rig Veda might perhaps be seen as vaguely parallel to the psalms, with which they share a roughly contemporaneous origin.

Interest in the Mahabharata has undergone a re-emphasis recently in Asian culture, but each family will have its own particular emphasis on certain texts which are held as superior to others. (In Ram's own family the *Ramayana* and *Gita* were held in particular esteem.)

Hindu texts are often scarce on information which teaches how to relate to normal human beings, or on teachings which relate to everyday life. You can learn how an officer should relate to his soldiers, but not how the average Hindu should relate to the person next door! Some texts are very esoteric, and most Hindus cannot understand what they have read, reading out of a sense of duty, rather than for comprehension.

Very few Hindus are directly familiar with any of these enigmatic texts, which are very long and wordy. More importantly, few Asians have the time or inclination to read any of them, because they are not 'user-friendly' books; hence the need for professional help - priests and *gurus* to teach other Hindus about what they say. (Christianity had the same problem in medieval times, when the Bible was published only in Latin and the common people had to depend on the priests' interpretations.) There has been no real reformation in Hinduism, which might deliver the faith back into the hands of the common people. Reform movements such as Buddhism, Jainism and Sikhism have sadly ended up 'outside the fold', as separate socio-religious groupings. *Gurus* and *brahmins* are still strongly relied upon as religious authority figures by the average Hindu family.

The original texts are in Sanskrit, and English translations are not valid for prayer, because the sounds of the words are very important. Second generation immigrants are often totally unfamiliar with Sanskrit and other Asian tongues. The texts are very rare and expensive to purchase. There is only one definitive version of each text and that's it. There are not dozens of different translations, as there are for the Bible; few commentaries; and no daily devotions. At the popular end of the market, comic versions are available of the Mahabharata, but no middle-ground theological teaching. A plateful of **Karma 'n' Chips** may help to bridge this gap!

The issue for Hindus is not whether they *understand* scriptures; the simple crux is that it's an esoteric icon. You can't derive Hindu theology from the exotic Hindu scriptures in the way that Christian theology can be derived from the Bible - attempting to do so has led many well-meaning Christians up many a blind alley! One strand of Hindu scriptures will guide you to the conclusion that Hinduism is monistic, and another will lead to pantheist conclusions. Everything is relative and nothing is absolute. Much is perplexing and contradictory. Hindu scriptures have to be approached with a different mind set if they are to be understood, though few Hindus even bother to try. Hindu scriptures have no more impact on the daily activity of the average Hindu than the Bible has on the life of most non-Christians or nominal believers.

Those who do read and understand are often troubled by their understanding. There is a story told in the book *Death of a Guru*, about one Hindu whose reading of the scriptures nearly led him to kill his aunt! In Ayodhya, a pile of rubble where a mosque once stood - and 1,100 graves throughout India - offer mute testimony to the actions of certain zealous Hindus whose view of their religion lead them into an orgy of death and destruction.

If the proof of the pudding is in the eating, then some people would conclude that the pudding has been spiked with something very unpleasant. Let's see if we can find where the corruption set in...

PART ONE: THE BOW IS DRAWN

'God has no religion.'
- Mahatma Gandhi

CHAPTER

1

DHARMA: *What on earth is my duty?*

If there has been one single factor responsible for the precious stability of South Asian families over the last three thousand years or so, it is the social and religious concept of family duty or *dharma*.

For fully 20% of the world's population, in India and its environs, and for the estimated ten million expatriate Asians now scattered across the globe, *dharma* has been the 'glue' that has drawn together the disparate factions of Asian society.

Every moment, somewhere in the world, an Asian is explaining to a quizzical non-Asian that sons, sons-in-law and widow(er)s all have specific duties to perform, or *dharma* to meet, at particular stages in life. For example, it is the duty of a Hindu male child to look after his parents in their old age, because that is his *dharma*. It is the son's sacred duty to ensure that the funeral of his parents is correctly carried out. A son-in-law's duty, of course, is to look after the daughter; but really the duty operates the other way, with the son-in-law having to be provided for, and properly respected over and above the sons of the family. The dowry system also often operates more to the benefit of the son-in-law than anyone else:

Daughters in a family, must have a dowry when they marry; it is their father's *dharma* to provide it. Going to the temple and donating money for its running is a religious duty or *dharma*. It's like an unwritten set of law which all Asians have to keep. It has got to be done, or the family will lose its *izzat*: its dignity, its pride and its respected place within the community.

Dharma means to keep faithfully to the Asian culture into which you were born, because it is that which gives you value, meaning and purpose. To deny or betray your culture, by not providing for your children, or by ignoring your parents, is to deny your *dharma* and to bring disrepute upon yourself and your family. (It also contributes to your bad *karma*, but that is a concept for a later chapter.)

What drives a westerner to work is a desire for self improvement, to earn a living and to bring up the family. The goal is a nice house, a nice car and a nice wife. For Asians too there is an aspect of providing for the family and keeping in line with the expectations of the society within which he or she moves. But Asians are more inclined to operate for the *extended* family's benefit, perhaps by creating businesses that will provide not just for the children but for the grandchildren, while the westerner is more orientated towards 'self'.

Ram Chandra Gupta, in *The Wonder that is Hindu Dharma*, says: 'Hindu *dharma*, and the eager pushful young who are keen on worldly success... Dharma was created for regulating the human conduct for the progress and welfare of society...'

But how does this age-old system work out in lands far from the native Indian soil which nurtured them? *After World War II, literally millions of Asians flocked to Britain, Australia, South Africa and other western countries. While many succeeded financially, they faced a profound culture shock as they grappled with differences in language, climate, food, clothing and attitudes. The children of these immigrants are often more at home in the host culture than that of their ethnic background, and the resulting stresses and strains can be unbearable.* How then, is the western Asian to execute his or her *dharma* in a country where the whole concept of duty has an entirely different meaning?

The British Asian newspaper *Eastern Eye* occasionally publishes agony columns, and even editorial comments, where the action of a particular individual is described as 'not good izzat'. Though *izzat* is a concept not exclusive to Hinduism - Muslims use it too - its use in a western newspaper indicates that Asian values have not been completely thrown out of the window by expatriate Asian communities. Yet the frequency with which Asians are marrying outside of their community, even to white westerners, indicates that traditional values are beginning to break down.

The diminution of the now unspoken caste system, and the increased dignity of the individual to marry whoever he or she please, are no bad things. But there are cases of elderly parents being left to fend for themselves in a country where even the language is a stranger to them. The attempted suicide rate amongst young Asian women in Britain has risen sharply, poignantly reflecting a deep level of dissatisfaction about the way *dharma* has become an increasingly difficult conception to execute adequately and competently. Disgrace has become a too-frequent visitor to too many homes of western Asians, and the immediate future does not look too welcoming.

Western 'Dharma'

Dharma is a strict moral code similar to the unwritten 'codes of conduct' that have prevailed in the West for perhaps as long as *dharma* has dominated the Asian way of life. In Britain, for example, it is traditional that the bride's father should always pay for the wedding; though tradition often takes a back seat these days, with the bride and groom dipping into their own pockets, too.

Before the war, it was 'unheard of' for a western woman to go out to work once she was married. It would have been a social disgrace - almost immoral - for her not to stay at home looking after the house and raising children while the husband worked to support the family. Since the liberating 1960s, when there was more work available than there were men to do it, it has become first 'accepted' and then 'the norm' for women to go out to work for a large portion of their lives.

The 1960s brought with it a relaxation of discipline in the west. Children had much more freedom, as it became trendy for them to be allowed fuller 'self-expression' while growing up. Sometimes this fashonable freedom was abused, becoming a licence for young people to do as they pleased, with no thought of responsibility or duty to parents or society in general. The birth control pill led to two decades of widespread promiscuity until the fear of contracting AIDS forced restraint upon sexual lifestyles.

The closest western equivalents of *dharma*, then, have changed radically over the past fifty years, due to changes in modern society. Divorce has become much easier; in Britain nearly one in three marriages - and in America one in two - end in divorce. A hundred years ago, divorce was a social disgrace which occurred infrequently because only the rich and powerful could afford to divorce - the procedure was outside the jurisdiction of the courts, and each divorce required the individual consent of Parliament.

Many western Asians are integrating themselves into societies where former social taboos are now being broken with gay abandon. For many Asians, *dharma* is becoming replaced with a new code of life: *individual freedom at all costs*. We can be sure that the role of *dharma* is not going to grow in importance in the west in the foreseeable future. Young Asians and westerners alike are aboard a runaway locomotive, the moral constraints which acted as brakes are failing fast; there may be a sharp turn ahead - another catastrophe worse than AIDS - and perhaps the train will not be able to stop in time. Our cultural background or skin colour will not save us from the carnage.

Decline into Anarchy

For nearly two thousand years, western society was built on the firm foundation of Christian values. The *Holy Bible* provided a reliable framework of moral standards and absolute values based upon the character of God himself. In the 1990s, that concept is enough to raise a chuckle from most Asians! What kind of a God is this whose values and character have given rise to a society where crime and lawlessness are rampant, and a woman is not safe to be outdoors by herself at night. In Britain, unemployment has claimed three million victims for a whole decade, and the newspapers are full of murders, rapes, adultery and corruption in high places. *Is this God a perverted madman?*

No, there is a better explanation: The decline of moral standards has coincided with the decline in church attendance in the west. As Christianity has become marginalised, society has slipped into anarchy. The industrial revolution of the nineteenth century took people away from agriculture and the natural harmony of the seasons, imposing in their place man-made structures which left God out of the picture. It took Christian social reformers - such as Shaftesbury, Wilberforce and Muller - to end slavery and to fight for the rights both of children forced to work down coal mines, and of men labouring in factories for fourteen hours per day.

Meanwhile in India, the British empire brought peace, a prosperous economy, transport and communications to a once-free India that had become wracked with petty feudalism, its political structure eradicated by centuries of alien domination. Yet, as Europe's emancipating technology steadily reached India throughout the ninteenth century, the sub-continent's self-sufficiency became slowly eroded. Bureaucratic machinery gradually deposed the autonomy and humane co-operation with which the colonial era had commenced. By the early twentieth century, Europeans were felt to have largely outstayed their welcome in India. It is significant that the decline of Asian respect for Europeans, and the intrusiveness of foreign domination, coincided with the ascent of godlessness in the European homelands. Sadly, the compassionate missionaries were lumped in with the ruthless government officials.

Once, many westerners performed good deeds because they felt it was their duty to God to behave charitably and compassionately, following the example of Jesus Christ. Some might have performed charitable duties to earn a better place in the next life, but gradually the religious connotations became irrelevant, as Christianity became isolated in the rising tide of secularism. Now, westerners are more likely to be charitable out of a sense of guilt acrued from the often ruthless way in which they earn their money. For others, charity becomes more a question of honour - not necessarily honour for its own sake, but for the prestige, social connections and rewards which come from their peer group believing them to be wealthy!

Fortunately, there are still many Christians in the west - constituting perhaps 3-4% of the population - for whom their faith is not simply nominal, and who remain committed to the person and ideals of Jesus Christ, striving to make them real within the modern world. For them, 'God' is not a swear word. Struggling to be like salt and light in a society that has lost its savour and that is enveloped in spiritual darkness and moral decay, Christian believers are the equivalent of *brahmin* priests, studying the scriptures and seeking to put them into practice. It is now not uncommon for ordinary Christians to exercise teaching and pastoral roles that might once have been reserved for a minister of religion. The western church has moved inexorably towards an every-person ministry where each believer is a priest.

Dharma on the Cosmic Stage

The idea that committment to a moral and ethically upright lifestyle comes as a result of religious belief is not a new concept to Asians because, of course, *dharma* has strong religious connotations. Easterners see God in every aspect of life; the sacred and profane are not separated, and daily rituals become unobtrusively significant. *Dharma* is at the very heart of the Asian religions. Morality and ethics are writ large in many of the sacred texts which undergird a Hindu's faith.

'No word is more important or more omnipresent in the sacred texts, yet those very texts warn us time and time again that this *dharma* is "subtle" and "difficult to know",' says Professor Zaehner in his classic study. 'Indeed, it is the very ambivalence of this key concept that both gives to Hinduism its distinctive flavour and sets up within it a tension that is never fully resolved.'

Part of the problem lies with *dharma* having two 'types' of meaning. The *dharma* we have considered up to now is dharma as it affects the individual, in the sense of being a duty to perform. About this, the Hindu texts are quite clear, and detailed. In the *Bhagavad Gita*, for example: 'Better to do one's own duty though void of merit, than to do another's duty however well performed. Doing the works that inhere in one's own condition one remains unsullied.' (*18.47*)

Yet there is a second type of *dharma*, the duty which holds not merely humans but the whole universe in its thrall. This cosmic *dharma* comprises the unfathomable ordinances of nature which govern the universe - including the laws of space and time. Taken to extremes time is seen as Fate, weaving an inescapable web about the affairs of whole castes and races. This *dharma* is 'the form of things as they are, and the power that keeps them that way'. Fatalism and superstition now run through all of Hindu society. One British Asian gives the following example:

'When my wife was expecting our first child, we received a phone call from a member of our extended family saying that astrologically a certain day was ill-omened. "Be careful that your wife does not sew on that day in case she pricks her finger and harms the baby"! As Christians, we ignored the admonishment; but it's typical of the kind of superstitious advice which many Hindu families would have heeded for fear that the wife would prick herself and harm the baby.'

Astrology is an influential factor in choosing a child's name. Perhaps an astrologer will indicate that he hears a particular vowel sound which ought to be part of the baby's name.

Sanatana Dharma

Dharma is an abstract expression of morality. It has a wide range of meanings, such as law, truth, teaching, righteousness, morality and duty. It is also a person's conscience.

'In the Upanishads, God is considered morally pure, free from all evil, whose nature is to bring righteousness and repel evil,' says Mariasusai Dhavamony in his text *Classical Hinduism.* 'The morally good man is one who reproduces the divine model in himself. Ritual duties are given a spiritual meaning and the real sacrifice is that which is found in austerity, generosity, righteousness, non-injury and truthfulness... When one is passionately attracted to earthly goods, one is on the lower stages of spirituality and morality. The positive aspect of detachment is attachment to the Supreme reality,' by which Dhavamony means God.

Three central truths of the eternal law, the *sanatana dharma* are:
1) God exists.
2) People can come to know Him.
3) The whole purpose of life is to come to know God

This will come as a surprise to many Christians who will realise, perhaps for the first time, that both Hinduism *and* Christianity are founded upon these same three precepts!

There are, of course, different perceptions about *how* people can come to know God, and we will explore these in the middle part of **Karma 'n' Chips.**

Ram Chandra Gupta says that **sanatana dharma** 'gives a message for the entire human race for its unity and welfare. If one attempts to peek into the real spirit of dharma, one will realise that it aims at refining the human life with all the world over, by washing out the impurities of human mind, without which the ideal of unity and progress of the human race cannot be possibly obtained.

'The highest life enjoyed by dharma is what follows naturally from vital faith in the reality of God. If the indwelling of God in man is the highest truth, conduct which translates it into practice is the highest conduct.' Hindus and Christians alike can agree to this.

Back To Earth

The interaction between the cosmic scenario of *sanatana dharma*, and the earthy *dharma* which affects the daily lives of nearly a billion people is subtle. The way it bestows dignity, meaning and purpose is complex, and dependant upon heavy use of mythical allegory. For those not familiar with life on the sub-continent, an illustration is needed:

One example is that of modern ferrymen whose dignity comes from the actions of an earlier ferrymen, whose good deed in ferrying the god Rama across a river is recorded in the *Ramayana*. Hindus derive value from the deeds and actions of their forebears in a way which the western mind could never grasp. An occupation is noble because of the noble people who have done it in the past.

The downside is that deplorable occupations are elevated. Take temple prostitution, which still goes on in a big way in India. This disreputable profession - which many young girls take up out of economic necessity - gains a bogus dignity out of the action of Krishna in associating with many women in the Hindu texts.

Temple prostitution, child marriage, enforced widowhood, and encouraging women to throw themselves on their husband's funeral pyre were practices that greatly shocked eighteenth century Europeans.

In *The Soul of India*, Amaury de Riencourt writes, 'Some westerners, repelled by the more gruesome aspects of Hinduism, saw in India only a conglomeration of pagan sects addicted to the most barbaric customs; others, with a more or less pseudo-mystical bent, saw in India the land of eternal wisdom and the fount of a world-wide spiritual revival of the future. Nowhere was there an attempt to look at India from both angles at once, to see objectively that Indian history conformed to a definite pattern of history but that, at the same time, Indian civilization had a unique personality of its own and could not be judged by (western) standards.'

If westerners looked at Hindu belief and practice with eastern eyes, they would see that the *dharma* concept in particular has much to commend it. It is a moral code of conduct which holds together the extended family, and overflows into broader social concern. When you see the moral fabric of the west in a state of decay - with the Christian values which long sustained pride and decency now ignored by much of the population, while corruption, greed and breakdown in family life threaten the very heart of western society - then the west comes to appear as pagan and barbaric as many Asian customs looked to the first Europeans who arrived in India!

Spiritual values are important for the moral and ethical progress of any society, but they need to be constantly re-defined to be made appropriate and to remain culturally relevant within an evolving social order.

Where the *dharma* system operates there are strong bonds of concern, family care and community spirit. Each community member cares for the others in a powerfully beneficial way. Destitution is held at bay by other family members rallying around. Kinship is given a high status; the concern for reputation brought by a sense of *dharma* is similar to that found in parts of the Holy Bible.

It often comes as a surprise for many Asians when they find how culturally relevant the Judaeo-Christian scriptures can be to their own situation. In the Bible book of *Ruth*, for example, we encounter a mother and daughter-in-law situation with which Asian families are intimately familiar. The girl's husband has died, but she doesn't want to leave the extended family into which she has married, so her mother-in-law - *after some scheming that would not be out of place in an Asian feature film!* - fulfils her dharma and arranges for her faithful daughter-in-law to marry another kinsman; and they all live happily ever after.

Looking Ahead

How, though, can traditional Asian religious duties be interpreted and discharged in a land where most of the population hold entirely different beliefs? Where possible, many families try to preserve everything exactly as it was in India, though they don't always succeed. Take temple duties, for example: In India, these would always take place on a particular day, but greater flexibility is required in the west. The pace of life in the west is chiefly responsible, but away from the motherland of Hindu culture, many of the rituals are beginning to lose their connotations and significance - particularly for second generation immigrants.

Those who believe that doing a 'duty to a god' by cleaning an idol will earn them bonus points in heaven, find that time is too short and life taken up by so many other chores to complete, that they cannot do enough of the religious duties. Formal expressions of belief begin to fall by the wayside, under the pressure of modern life. A move towards following the teachings of *gurus* often results from the scarcity of time for temple duties.

Dharma as a concept has been subjected to severe questioning in recent years, both in the west where it often seems at odds with western lifestyle, and in an increasingly modern India where many families have been exposed to strong western influences.

Voices that have been silenced for many years are beginning to speak about issues that have long been taboo in the Asian communities abroad. Early in 1994, the feature film *Bhaji on the Beach* stunned many families with its lewd plot revolving around three generations of Asian women on a day trip to a British seaside resort. They carry with them a complex set of social problems, ranging from single parenthood to domestic violence. Asians have been outraged by one scene featuring an unmarried Asian girl, pregnant by her black boy friend, staggering into a temple and lighting a cigarette from a sacred candle. Other scenes show Asian women drinking and dancing in a way said to present a bad example to the younger generation. What is *dharma* to mean in a society where these activities are becoming the norm for many Asians?

Austin Creel says, 'the attack on traditional formulations of *dharma* has not been merely logical or forensic; the introduction of new economic, political and social institutions has simply supplanted the traditional *dharma* in many areas of life.' A new equilibrium is needed.

In times of transition, people often struggle to find their roots in order to give themselves stability. The age old questions come to the fore. 'Who *am* I really?' is asked by some. 'Why am I here?' is an abstract puzzle to many others. When self-esteem has taken a hammering, they ask 'Am I of value? And if so, why? And to whom?'

The status of an Asian's family determines the individual's prestige in society. One western Asian, Sunil, gives an example: 'I met someone at a High Commissioner's function who asked me where I came from and whose son I was. It transpired that he had known my father forty years ago. I was suddenly elevated in his eyes because he realised that mine was a wealthy and prestigious family.' On another occasion, when a man realised that Sunil's aunt was an affluent and influential lady, Sunil was immediately offered a very lucrative business deal. The man kept saying, 'I can offer you this deal because I know that you are not a cowboy, you come from a good family.'

To answer the more abstract questions, people often turn to religion. Hindus are fond of celebrating the milestones in their lives with devotional ceremonies, where symbols are used to expound great religious truths. For many 'life landmarks' the symbolism is about all that is left. In some families, these have a social but no sacred significance; some families have abandoned rituals altogether; sometimes the ceremonies take place in secret while other families have them out in the open. There is no standard practice.

Though traditionally Asians have turned to their *brahmin* priests for the answers to moral and spiritual questions, in the west at least, Hindu priests are in short supply and few of them are able to offer any answer which is even vaguely satisfactory for the educated Indian. It is becoming increasingly important for individuals to work out their spiritual views for themselves. But where to start?

You could always begin with God...

*'God places salt on our tongue
so that we thirst for him.'
- St Augustine.*

BRAHMAN: *What in heaven is God like?*

Hindu and Christian beliefs both point towards the same unfathomable mystery - the holiness and sanctity of eternal God himself. There may be differing views of which faith takes us closest, but ultimately neither faith can be more than a picture or model of the true reality which is the essence of the divine being.

The wise and the witty have all tried to understand God, and their views have ranged from the sublime to the ridiculous...

'If people stop believing in God, they don't believe in nothing, they believe in anything' - GK Chesterton.

'God is like a person who clears his throat while hiding and so gives himself away' - Meister Eckhardt.

'How can I believe in God when just last week I got my tongue caught in the roller of an electric typewriter?' - Woody Allen.

'God's a funky little dude because everyone's looking for him and no one can find him' - Prince.

On the surface, there appears to be little agreement over whether God is a unique entity, or just one of many spiritual beings. Conventional wisdom has it that Christianity is a monotheistic faith, while Hindu belief is polytheistic; but this is a gross over-simplification. It is commonly said that Christians worship a personal God while Hindus know only an impersonal 'force' called *Brahman*; but this too is inaccurate.

At first glance, there does indeed seem to be a veritable Mount Olympus of gods in the Hindu pantheon. The Vedic era knew Agni, Indra, Varuna, and a whole constellation of lesser gods. Some faded from importance and were replaced with others until - by the classical period - the three main gods worshipped with reverence and awe, were Brahma, Vishnu and Siva. Since then, Brahma has lost all importance, particularly in South India, and been replaced by Krishna and Rama - both said to be incarnations of Vishnu.

In *The Spirit of Hinduism*, anthropologist David Burnett has conveniently ranked the Hindu deities, both major and minor. Above all is Brahman (whom westerners must be careful not to confuse with *Brahma*, the creator god.) At a second level is the supreme reality embodied and worshipped as the devas, the pan-Indian deities such as Durga, Ganesha and Kali.

'Theoretically, individuals may choose to worship whichever deity they will. This is the teaching known as Ishtadeva,' says Burnett. 'Regarding the everyday life of the villagers, these second-level deities are not generally worshipped, as they are considered remote and preoccupied with running the universe.' This is particularly true of Hindus in remote villages, but in larger cities and in the west second level gods such as Krishna and Rama are very popular figures of devotion, alongside Vishnu and Siva who, together with Brahma make up a kind of Hindu 'trinity'.

The regional gods or *devatas* (godlings) are guardian deities who constitute an extraordinary medley of deified forces and natural phenomena, spirits of different diseases, and the ghosts of the dead. These godlings perhaps correspond to the powers and principalities, thrones and dominions of which the apostle Paul spoke in his 'thesis on spiritual warfare' in the book of *Ephesians*. Certainly they sound like the kind of spirits which many charismatic Christians claim to have occasionally encountered in daily life.

Burnett explains: 'Most of the *devatas* either have a specific function, or are associated with a particular group, and have the general function of serving as guardians to the village. An important class of devata is the female spirits called *matas*.' *Mata* means 'mother', and is an important cult with a following through many parts of India.'

At the fourth and lowest levels are the more localised spirits, demons and *bhuts*. *Bhut* means simply 'being' but, unlike *devas*, the *bhuts* are thought to have a direct and manifest affect on village affairs. They can cause distress, affliction and - in rare instances - the phenomenon of spirit possession. In some rites, *bhuts* are foolishly invited to ritually take over the body of one of the worshippers. The western equivalent would perhaps be a poltergeist, spirit or ghost; while the Muslim tradition might identify them as *jinn*.

Singularly Plural?

With all these spiritual beings within the Hindu spiritual dimension, it seems hard to argue that Hindus are not polytheistic. But there are two points that are usually missed.

Firstly, practising Hindus worship minor deities believing that they represent the one supreme deity whom they hold to be so remote and aloof as to be unreachable with worship. Instead, they find a minor deity to worship, who is nearer and approachable. Secondly, though many deities are devoutly worshipped (metaphorically at any rate, India has 330,000,000 gods) generally speaking, each individual Hindu worships just one deity exclusively.

The evocation of a minor spiritual being, in preference to the supreme deity, is also found in some Christian traditions! The Roman Catholic and the Eastern Orthodox traditions have both long set great store in prayers directed either to saints or to Mary the mother of Jesus. Prior to the Reformation early in the sixteenth century, the adoration of holy men whose merits had qualified them to be called saints, and the veneration of relics associated with these holy people during their earthly lives, played a major part in popular western faith, though it is not authentic to Bible-based Christianity.

In *Hinduism and Christianity*, Brockington laments 'the application of a double standard, whereby Christianity is judged at the level of its doctrinal formulations and Hinduism is judged by its day-to-day practice. If both were judged at the same level, the distinctions would not seem nearly as clear-cut.'

Even at the level of scripture, pure monotheism is not immediately apparent. Originally written in Hebrew, hardly have the Judaeo-Christian scriptures begun when the word 'God' makes an appearance - it's the third word of the first book - and the word used to denote God is *elohim*, a word meaning 'spiritual beings' in the plural! Jews craftily point out that in every sentence where *elohim* is used to denote God, other words are conjugated as though the noun was in fact singular. In a handful of instances, this linguistic contrivance, together with clues from the context, are the major indicators enabling the translators to know when the scriptures are speaking of the supreme being, rather than the lesser gods, or angelic beings.

Elsewhere, other words are used to denote almighty God, particularly the word *Yahweh*, his personal name; and *el*, usually used as a suffix to identify God by some title which describes the specific attributes being shown. Nevertheless, it is remarkable the way the very syntax of the Hebrew language is used to indicate that God is several persons within the one being...

The *trinity*, as it is called, can be a very tricky concept for anyone to grasp, so some like to use the 'red rubber ball' analogy. Just as Christians believe Father, Son and Holy Spirit are each entirely and completely God, full of infinite grace and mercy, so a red rubber ball is entirely red, entirely round and entirely made of rubber. The three characteristics are in no way contradictory. Each adds to our overall understanding of the object we are describing. Similarly the three persons of the *trinity* taken together give us a more complete idea of the enigmatic and inscrutably infinite Godhead than each on his own. Another analogy might be that the trinity is like steam, water and ice - all superficially different, but chemically identical.

(Divine mathematics can tentitively be glimpsed by earthly mathematicians. A young child knows that the sum $1+1+1=1$ does not add up properly. But it takes a more knowledgable mathematician to realise that infinity + infinity + infinity can have no value other than infinity...)

Plurally Singular

At the very core of Christianity, believers worship three persons in one godhead, believing God the Father, God the Son, and God the Holy Spirit to be co-eternal, of one being and majesty. The idea that Father, Son and Holy Spirit are *not* three separate deities has never been well understood by people from the east. Jews and Muslims alike are outraged at what they see as a threat to God's uniqueness. Islam denounces Christians for the heresy of *shirk* in equating Jesus with the one God who is without equal. If a worldwide survey were carried out to see how many people believed Christianity to be monotheistic, the faith would probably get less than 50% of the votes!

One problem particularly for Asians in understanding the idea of the *trinity* is that there is no word in any of the Asian languages that is the accurate equivalent of 'person'. The closest equivalent word means 'individual'. It is therefore impossible to communicate the idea to a Hindu in any Asian tongue that 'God is three persons in one Godhead'. Attempts will always tend to sound as though there are three individual gods representing a greater supreme being - akin to Brahma, Vishnu and Siva representing Brahman - and incompatible with strict monotheism!

Though Father, Son and Holy Spirit are all regarded as fully sharing in the divinity of the Godhead, God also 'manifests' himself physically in ways which seem to involve less than the whole of his divinity. In several places we encounter the Angel of the Lord, or the 'commander of the army of the Lord', who accepts the worship and honour due to God: Joshua falls prostrate at his feet and is not rebuked for it (Joshua 5:14). Yet the fullness of God cannot be present in this manifestation, because the Bible says elsewhere that no one has seen ineffable God's awesome face and lived.

Perhaps the most mysterious person in the whole Bible is Melchizedek, king of Salem, priest of God Most High. He behaves in an esoteric Christ-like manner, offering Abraham bread and wine. It is said of Melchizedek by the author of a part of the Bible called the book of *Hebrews* that he is 'without father or mother, without genealogy, without beginning of days or end of life, like the Son of God he remains a priest forever'. (*Hebrews 7:3*) He 'has become a priest not on the basis of a regulation as to his ancestry but on the basis of the power of an indestructible life.' (*Hebrews 7:16*) King David, who lived approximately a millenium after Abraham and a millenium before Christ, wrote cryptically, 'The Lord (*Yahwah*) says to my Lord... "You are a priest for ever, in the order of Melchizedek",' (*Psalm 110:1,4*).

It all points to Jesus Christ's pre-existence long before his earthly incarnation as Mary's son. Yet no Christian theologian has ever seriously suggested that Melchizedek or the Angel of the Lord share in the Godhead in the same way as Father, Son or Holy Spirit. *This is similar to the Hindu belief that the supreme being can be 'partly-present' in god-like forms where less than the fullness of his divinity is manifest.*

Hinduism has been accused of barbarism, particularly due to the violent acts of Siva, the god of destruction. Yet in the book of Exodus, God passes over the houses of the Egyptians and strikes down every firstborn, an action reflecting his right and willingness to punish the unrighteous, but as violent as any of the actions attributed to Siva...

Points of View

Little in religion is ever clear cut; but where God is concerned, trying to pin him down is like trying to unravel a conundrum wrapped within a paradox tied up with enigmas. Hindus and Christians alike struggle to understand what God is really like, and in everyday life the answers they arrive upon are often determined by presuppositions arising from home background, social class and local custom.

In Jaipur, a resident priest rings the temple bells each morning; washes the statues of the deities; then offers incense, flowers and food to the statues. The food is distributed as *prasad* to the local people who come to hear him recite formal prayers and join in the *bhajans* or sacred songs several times each day. Some will slip him a crumpled ten rupee note as he hands them a candle to wave before the idol of their choice, in the ceremony called *arti*.

The priest probably hasn't the foggiest notion of what God is like, whether he is one or many, and as long as worshippers continue to give him money to provide for his wife and three children he doesn't really care. The people who come to him are certain that these idols of wood and stone *are* the very gods themselves; so yes, of course, the view here may well be that there is more than one God.

In Bradford, Mr Patel rises early in the little flat above the bustling newspaper shop he owns. He has a quick bath, dresses, then hurries to his household shrine in the corner of the kitchen and lights a candle before a picture of his holy man, Sathya Sai Baba. This guru's gentle face topped with corkscrew hair gazes from the photograph as Mr Patel continues his *puja,* or worship, glad that he worships a divinity that has descended to earth in the form of this humble man. Of course God is singular and personal; here is his photograph to prove it!

Mrs Chaudhari lives with her husband and three children in a remote Indian village, in the foothills of the Himalayas. Rising in the tiny tin-roofed shack she calls home, she bathes as best she can with water from the cattle trough and hurries off to the squalid and ramshackle building which serves as a place of worship for the small community in which she lives. There, she lays the handful of flowers she has lovingly prepared on the top of the short pillar, or *lingam*, in Siva's shrine; then, muttering the prayers that her mother taught her by rote, she prostrates herself full length on the dirty floor as a gust of wind dislodges the flowers and sends them tumbling into the filthy water at the foot of the lingam. For her, God is so impersonal that even Siva who represents him has no human attributes. This abstract pillar which serves as his altar must serve as a symbol to the unknowable and frightening deity whom she hopes will grant her good luck in the day ahead.

Which of these three is a Hindu? They all are, of course! Hindus have total freedom of choice regarding the deity they worship and the method of the worship itself.

Popular books say that, for Hindus, the supreme deity, Brahman, is impossibly distant and 'abstract' with no human attributes through which he may be known; not at all like the intimately personal and knowable God worshipped by Christians. He is more a force than a person - a universal absolute, as inscrutable as an abstract mathematic equation and as remote as a distant galaxy. But these statements are too sweeping and this scenario is too glib; there are too many exceptions in everyday practice for this rule to be entirely true.

Case for the Abstract

Almighty and majestic God would seem to be revealed, in diverse times and places, in both a personal way and through abstract symbols. Most Christians, though, would refute that God is ever impersonal; transcendent, distant and invisible he may be, but there is plenty of indication that God is always intensely personal.

Early in the Bible, there are instances of God speaking with the first man, Adam, as they walked in the cool of the day. The patriarch Enoch, too, is described as having 'walked with God'; and Abraham received a visit from God as he was sitting at the entrance of his bedouin tent. These appearances would seem though to have been of God in less than his fulness - no one can see the face of God and live, according to the Judaeo-Christian scriptures. (Exodus 33:23)

On the other hand, in the Bible, there are points where eternal God is shown, not through the persons of the trinity, but distantly, through abstract symbolism. The confrontation between God and his people at Mount Sinai is one example. Here, God is so remote and mysterious that he refuses to allow the people to approach him, remaining obscured in cloud atop a mountain, promising to strike dead anyone who touches the mountain, let alone tries to climb up.

Only God's chosen one, Moses, is allowed to climb to the

Varuna had been seen as the sovereign ruler of the gods - divinity with a personal face - but with the sacred power seen to lie not with 'the gods' but *with the sacrifice itself.* Gradually, the gods became marginalised and the sacrifices came to be seen as *ways of controlling spiritual powers.* The Brahmin priests evolved into sorcerers, casting spells and chanting to gain authority over spiritual forces. It was an age of magicians.

The Upanishads (written circa 1000-500BC) tentatively moved the emphasis once again - away from the sacrifice and focusing on Brahman the absolute. The early Upanishads identify Brahman either as food, as breath, or as both. Early in the Jewish scriptures, the *Torah* speaks of the creative Spirit of God, and the Hebrew word translated as spirit (*ruah*) is also the word meaning breath, or wind. The Koran's title for Jesus is Ruh-Allah, meaning 'spirit/breath of God'. In the Christian scriptures, wind, breath and spirit are all denoted by the same word in the original Greek. There would seem, therefore, to be a common source for the belief in God as breath.

Perhaps Jews and Hindus, casting around for a way to describe the awesome mystery of God, hit upon the concept of breath/wind to capture his elusiveness. (But perhaps God is not really either of those; they are only metaphors seeking to describe someone too awesome and mysterious for us to grasp in actuality.)

The Upanishads begin to explore the *implications* of believing God to be *non-personal* - not in the sense of having no personality, but of transcending personality and being somehow 'suprapersonal' or (to use theologian Paul Tillich's term) transpersonal. The Upanishads certainly don't put forward a single coherent viewpoint, any more than the theological and philosophical thoughts of Christian writers down the ages always converge in a single point.

The early Upanishads tend to favour the idea of God being impersonal, while the later Upanishads generally favour a personal God, but both views can be found throughout the whole era when the Upanishads were written. Some see Brahman itself as personal, but generally *Isvara* is taken as the personal essence of the divinity, and *Brahman* as the impersonal.

'Brahman is so immutable and unmanifest, beyond every capacity for action, that Isvara has to take over its functions in relation to the universe,' says Panakkar.

The unique relationship between *Brahman* the transcendent and unknowable absolute, and *Isvara* the personal God, is bewildering in its complexity. The Christian *trinity* is perhaps one unexpected answer to this affinity between the absolute and the relative, as we shall later see. *Isvara* can perhaps be seen as 'the all-powerful God on whom the theistic tendencies of the Upanishads converge'.

The word *Isvara* does not occur in the Rig Veda, nor is there any clear distinction between abstract Brahman and personal Isvara in the earliest Upanishads. Towards the end of their period of composition, however, the idea of a personal God had tentatively emerged - as it were - from the shadow of the unknowable absolute. Isvara is said to be 'Brahman seen through

Just as steam cannot be seen unless it condenses into water or freezes into ice, *Brahman* cannot be known unless revealed in the tangible form of Isvara. It has been said that *Brahman* is God in passive mode, and *Isvara* reflects an active mode, but the truth may be simply unknowable. (We will try to reconcile all these views in the next chapter.)

Traveller's Tales

Again, whether God is seen as personal or abstract - or the point where an individual believer places God on a semantic scale between the two extremes - is largely determined by individual upbringing and cultural background. When Mike Fearon was in India researching Karma'N'Chips, he encountered a wide variety of views:

Inside the temple to Kali in Calcutta, a talkative *brahmin* priest explained that in his view all the different gods were personal and composed a sort of Parliament, yet the supreme God was an impersonal being. 'The different gods are controlling one natural power. Here at the Kali temple, you worship that natural power through different gods. To save us from the fire we worship Brahma, because he controls the fire. If we worship Siva, we will get sound health for a long life. We worship God under different names for different purposes and different expectations. Kali we worship here, to fight the devil power of the world. If we get the blessing of the goddess Kali, we can fight over all the devils. She cuts off the heads of the devils and kills them all. She is a blessing to the world.'

Are these 'devils' abstract forces like jealousy and pride, or are they persons? 'Yes, they are forces. The common people don't understand this, though. We, the *brahmin,* we understand these things.' Yes, but *brahmins* understand the same things in different ways, and each priest seems to have his own interpretation. This particular priest was ready at one moment to say that God and gods are both abstract, and the next instant to describe the gods as personal! More concerned with blagging a donation for temple funds than in maintaining the integrity of his theological reasoning, he promptly conceded every religious argument in which he and Mike engaged...

At Allahabad, where the sacred river Ganges meets the river Yamuna, pilgrims arrive from all over India to bathe in the waters, and then go to the temple of the monkey god Hanuman with sacrifices. Hanuman shares the temple with an effigy of Ganesha the elephant god, so someone clearly believed that both gods were representatives of a single entity - but personal or impersonal? 'Attitude is very important,' explained one leather-skinned holy man or *sadhu*, sitting in the lotus position at the temple's entrance. 'People come here with an attitude, and ask God to do something for them - perhaps they are childless and want a child.' He too seemed very unsure about his own beliefs, though he considered God to be sufficiently personal that he can be petitioned with requests.

Asked for his view of God, he replied agnostically: 'Because we are doing this, there must be some fruit or consequence. We don't know how worship works but there should be a way.' All around, people were prostrating themselves on the dank floor, walking around the effigy of the monkey god, or sitting quietly and reading sacred texts. For them, God seemed to be very personal. 'If you believe that this effigy is a god, then it is a god,' the *sadhu* said, evidently content that people should self-hypnotise themselves into believing anything they wanted. He saw belief to be a personal matter; if people want to believe God is personal, that is alright; if they want to believe he is abstract, then that is alright too.

Muslims believe that, though awesome in his majesty, God is sufficiently personal that he can be referred to as 'he' rather than 'it'; his transcendence is so great that he is seen as acting impersonally, but his righteousness and separation from the created order make him appear capricious. Clearly there is a similar problem as in Christian and Hindu beliefs, in trying to define the ambiguous nature of holy God - though Islamic interpretations tend to be very fatalistic. Muslims are adamant that God is one person and in no way a parliamant or trinity; this strict distinction is the major cause of tension between Hindus and Christians on one hand,

and Muslims on the other.

Case for the Personal

Hindu and Christian understanding of God are far from identical, and both are equally problematic for Muslims! A good deal of misunderstanding has been caused by two faiths using the word 'personal' with different meanings. The sanskrit word *purusha* does not have the same connotations as the latin *persona*, though each gives rise to the idea of the personal in eastern and western cultures respectively. Limitation is taken as implied by the word 'person' when it should not be. As Christian theologian Karl Barth has said, 'God is personal, but personal in an incomprehensible way, in so far as the conception of his personality surpasses all our views of personality.'

If having a personality implies that God is therefore limited, then perhaps he is self-limited in order that we might catch a glimpse of something too awesome that in an unlimited form would leave us dumbstruck, or drive us insane by his incomprehensible magnitude.

Vishal Mangalwadi does not accept that being infinite and being personal are mutually exclusive categories: 'In geometry, for example, we talk of an infinite straight line. If a line can be infinite and not include everything in it, then why can't God be infinite and not include everything within him? Just as a line is infinite within the limitations of what it is, so also God can be infinite within the limitation of that which He is.

'Christ's devotees also argue that in fact the concept of God as infinite-personal alone is credible. Because if God is impersonal He offers no basis for the value of the human personality. If He is finite... then He is not sufficient to carry philosophical unity as a universal being. The failure of finite deities becomes obvious in Greek and Hindu mythologies. Not only are there flaws in their character but there is always the confusion of whether fate is behind the gods or the gods behind fate. Also only a personal God can provide a basis for true morals.'

Culture Shock

Many people can't easily articulate their religious problems.

They think that suddenly to conceive almighty God as personal, when previously they believed him to be an abstract force - or vice versa - is like saying that two plus two suddenly equals five. *A Hindu suddenly claiming to understand God in a Christian way can seem like someone saying that they have turned into a teapot!* Have they 'transcended the limits of metaphysical exploration'? Or are they simply 'a pinch of cumin powder short of a curry'?

Coming to believe that perhaps Brahman is not the way you always thought he/it was is as radical as discovering that the earth revolves around the sun when previously you thought the reverse was true! Another Copernican revolution needs to take place, if Asians are going to become accustomed to the religious climate of the west - not because they don't understand the faiths of the west, but because they don't fully understand even the baffling complexities of their own ancestral faith. Christian and Hindu beliefs about God are not completely equatable, but there are enormous differences too *within* each tradition. No two Hindus necessarily share identical views about the equivocal nature of the supreme deity.

Finding other ways of looking at God doesn't mean that all the culture which went with the old way is wrong and must be dismissed. Faith and culture are not one homogenous unit, and changes in faith need not affect the way a person relates to his family or Asian culture in general.

When a group of Christian children were taken by their Asian father to see a squalid temple in Rishikesh, they were shocked and alarmed by what they saw. Instead of sitting on pews facing the front - as would have been the case in a church - the worshippers were sitting on the floor. Instead of keeping their shoes on, everyone was expected to go barefoot. There was no organ music, for here sitar and tablas were the normal accompaniment. The children were frightened by the lack of familiarity, and their father had to convince them that there was nothing to fear about the unfamiliar environment. Nothing in these purely cultural trappings would have needed to change if the priests had suddenly become Christians. Religion is not *dependent* upon culture - or vice versa - though popular culture is often a vehicle for expression and comment about religious faith.

Ram remembers, for example, in the film *Ek Phool Char Kante* (One Flower and Four Thorns) he saw a girl offering flowers and praying to an idol. She was speaking in such a personal way to an abstract piece of carved stone that it was difficult to be sure whether she was praying to a personal or an intangible god.

Western culture also reflects pre-Christian traditions and other influences (often eastern). In films, God is often shown to be abstruse: You might see someone praying, and then there will suddenly be a bright light from the side, and angelic music playing on the soundtrack. In the film *Time Bandits,* God is presented both as a disembodied voice (sometimes seen coming from an equally disembodied head!) and in personal human form looking like an ordinary business-suited stockbroker...

There are independent traditions and folklore in South Asia and in the west which see nature as an abstract expression of God - or God as the personification of nature. Both are ways of merging the personal and the abstract. British schoolchildren at a young age are often told of 'mother nature', who brings the seasons around and causes the flowers to bloom. The adult equilvalent is the New Age belief in a 'Gaia' hypothesis, which states that the planet's 'biosphere' - the sum total of all the life in the sea, on the surface and in the air - constitutes a single organism, a kind of earth mother or mother goddess. Goddess worship, of course, is very prevalent in India, where the Shakti cults are very popular. *In all these cases, a personal deity is seen as represented by the impersonal workings of the natural world.*

Within many Asian homes, the husband is seen as a symbolic representative of God. Many Asian pop songs speak of pati brahman, pati Vishnu, pati paramatman, depicting the head of the household as the model of an intensely personal deity. When Ram Gidoomal was a Cambridge examiner in Hinduism, the model answers he used when marking 'A' level GCE papers expected that successful candidates would say, 'in all cases the supreme being is described in the Upanishads as more or less personal'.

The Absolutely Personal God

The way in which people conceive of God affects the way in which they relate to him. We have seen some of the different views of God within Hindu and Christian traditions - and within traditions respectively older and more recent than either. Some views are very close, even identical. Pannikar suggests audaciously that Isvara and Christ may be the same:

'Isvara does all *for* and *as* Brahman and consequently is different from but identical to Brahman,' Panikkar espouses, believing ultimately, 'that from which the World comes forth and to which it returns and by which it is sustained, that is Isvara, the Christ.'

He cunningly defends the startling identification of Isvara with Christ by pointing out that the role of Isvara in Hindu texts 'corresponds functionally' with the role of Christ in the Christian Gospel. But Hindu theology as a whole is not easy to equate with all of Christian theology, or vice versa. Take prayer for example:

For Hindus, prayer takes on something very different from its Christian significance. It is necessary to transfer the meaning of the theological term 'prayer' across the spiritual boundaries if we are to understand its different meaning to different people.

Hindus generally have no concept of prayer as a dialogue with God. Hindu prayer, of course, entails reciting a short and formularised ritual, called a *mantra*, which invokes certain spirits. There are different mantras with different spiritual connotations, and the most powerful is *Om*. Tone and intonation are clearly very important parts of the repetitous chanting. Other Hindu prayers comprise huge chunks of sanskrit recited by a priest. Intercessory prayers are also said by a priest, usually for a small payment! Hindu meditation is emptying the mind; Christian meditation is filling the mind with thoughts of God.

Mangalwadi cleverly makes the following point in *World of the Gurus*: If the chief distinguishing marks of personality 'are the ability to engage in rational, propositional communication and interpersonal relationships, then an isolated being can only be a sub-personal individual. Personhood has a subjective, objective and relational dimension. *One is sub-personal without all three of these dimensions.*

'If God has existed eternally as a unitarian individual without anyone with whom He can communicate, at best He can only be an unfulfilled person who needs to create other personal beings in order to love and communicate with them.

'Such a God who *needs* something outside of Himself, is not self-sufficient or autonomous and therefore cannot be the final Absolute in the universe. But if God has existed eternally as three persons in a mutual relationship of love and communication then He can be self-sufficient and autonomous.' *Logically, a personal God cannot exist* without *comprising two or more persons within the Godhead*.

The easiest way to understand the trinity is to watch it at work in creation...

'The imagination imitates,
it is the creative spirit that creates'
- Oscar Wilde.

CHAPTER
3

MAYA: *How did God make the world*

Theology can be such a tough subject with which to get to grips, that many people simply put it to one side, and get on with the jobs of making money and bringing up a family!

Mahesh Patel certainly thought this was a good idea. He had managed to avoid thinking about God all the way through college, and for the first ten years of his professional career as an accountant. Then came the moment he had been dreading. His young son came home from school fired up with all sorts of religious questions. What was God like? Where did he come from? Did he really run the world? Mahesh caught his breath sharply.

After rambling on for several minutes, he could begin to see that his son was less than convinced about his dear father's religious knowledge. The game was up! Being a good and conscientious father, Mahesh decided to take the bull by the horns and try to find some genuine answers to these troublesome questions. If he was to continue to command respect within his own home, he needed to come up with some good answers...

The nature of God is probably the thorniest and most discussed subject in the annals of human history. The second most discussed subject, particularly amongst theologians, scientists and philosophers, is probably the origin and nature of the universe. With a sigh, Mahesh Patel decided that he had better go to his local library and do some reading.

The two subjects, Mahesh discovered, are closely connected. There are two basic theories describing the connection between God and the world. First is *monism*, which suggests that both the creator God and the whole of his material universe are of the same essence; all is one, and one is all. The second view, *dualism*, postulates that, though majestic God created the universe, he is not part of it, and is completely different in his quintessential nature.

Christians mainly subscribe to the latter view. Hindus are liable to take either view, but usually neither! There is a long history of controversy amongst Hindus on this issue of *monism versus dualism*, and the idea that Hinduism is a purely monistic faith is another myth - like the 'fable' that all Hindus believe the world is just an ethereal illusion...

The word *maya*, often thought to mean 'illusion', actually denotes God's mysterious 'power in the world'. The precise nature of that unfathomable power, and the scope of its application, depends on which Asian philosopher you follow; only one stoic intellectual has proposed that the world is anything like illusory.

There are six basic schools of orthodox Hindu philosophy, all of which accept the authority of the Vedas: They are the Nyaya, Vaiseshika, Sankhya, Yoga, Mimamsa and Vedanta schools. *Vedanta* is easily the most popular amongst intellectuals. Its chief exponent was Sankara, whose views were *close* to being monist. The two other major exponents were Madhva, an out-and-out dualist; and Ramanuja, whose qualified non-dualism takes a middle ground.

Sankara Says...

Even with an expensive education and a good university degree behind him, Mahesh was finding it tough going - but he was determined to persist. In the last 1,200 years or so, Mahesh discovered, all Hindu thought about the created universe has been influenced to a greater or lesser extent by Sankara (686-720 AD) whose intellectual genius was to bring together apparently contradictory passages of the Upanishads and to make some sense of the discrepancies.

Sankara tentatively postulated two complementary levels of truth. The first is utterly 'other worldly' while the second describes the ordinary world of everyday existence. Thus, if two portions of the Upanishads seemed to contradict each other, it was because each was speaking at a different level. On the upper level of reality, transcendental and eternal, was the absolute, impersonal Brahman - though not completely devoid of attributes. Brahman possessed the three attributes of 'being', 'consciousness', and 'bliss', according to Sankara. On the lower level, temporal and personal, Brahman appeared as the creator God, Isvara - though he could be known and worshipped in other names.

From Sankara's viewpoint, the dualist notion that both God and the world are equally real presented a major problem. It meant that God was in danger of being 'squeezed out of the picture'. If God had already completed his task of creation and was now totally independent of it, he had become redundant. Sankara resolved the problem by proposing that God is ineffably more 'real' than creation, which is held in existence by God's divine power. In relation to the reality of God, whom he called 'the real of the real', the universe is so comparatively nebulous as to be little more than an illusion.

Philosophically, this is not pure monism, but *Advaita* - a wierd concept similar to (but clearly not identical with) monism. Sankara's exotic system is called *Advaita Vedanta*, where Vedanta literally means 'the end of the Vedas'. *Maya* originally signified the 'creative power of the Vedic gods', and Sankara simply redefined its nature. *Maya* has often been misunderstood and misquoted, for Sankara was not 'an illusionist'. He fully accepted that, at least on one level of reality, the world exists and evolves under the control of Isvara, the personal deity, who sustains it in existence.

The Christian philosopher Thomas Aquinas had a similar idea. Indeed, Christian philosophers had gotten around the problem to some extent in their own way by proposing that God *sustains* the world in continual existence by his creative fiat. But a possible consequence of this old approach is a blurring of the duality into an unresolved paradox where the two are simply 'separate but united'. European philosophers are generally poorer than Indian philosophers when it comes to metaphysics, and Aquinas's stance is a pseudo-dualism which for many people is not intellectually satisfying. To use a familiar British proverb, 'You can't have your cake and eat it!'

In *Thinking about Hindus*, Mahesh read: 'Maya is like a veil drawn between man and reality, which makes things seem different from what they are. So while the world is changing, reality does not change. Put it another way, the world is real enough from the human point of view, but from the divine point of view, it is not.' Because the world appears real to people, it blocks out the sublime reality of God from humanity's perception.

It's as though there is a one way mirror which enables God to influence the world, but prevents the world from affecting God's singular holiness. (You could say that in maya creation is fitted with a shield that protects the creator from the sins of the people who populate it.)

Other Hindu thinkers such as the philosopher Aurobindo have strongly criticised Sankara for his conception of *maya*, believing that it does not do justice to the world's worth. One humourous story has it that a Maharajah whom he was instructing played a prank on Sankara by having a wild elephant released in his path. The Maharajah noticed that it was a sufficiently real elephant that the philosopher took shelter up a tree.... Sankara supposedly said 'That was not me you saw flee from an elephant up a tree, but the appearance of me fleeing from an illusory elephant up an unreal tree!' *But this joke at Sankara's expense peniciously misrepresents Advaita Vedanta.*

'The general teaching of the Upanishads is not that the phenomenal world is unreal, as is sometimes supposed: it emanates from the Absolute as sparks are emanated from fire or as a spider's web is woven out of itself by the spider. The "mortal" and the "unformed" are as much part of the "partless" Brahman as are the "immortal" and the "unformed",' Professor Zaehner insists. Many others consider that Sankara's philosophy has been misinterpreted and his similies misunderstood by his critics.

Advaita Vedanta

This was all heavy going for poor old Mahesh, but if his older relatives could spend hours on end listening to the rambling teaching of *gurus*, he could surely spend hours reading up about his ancestral faith, and its relevance - if any - to the dynamic modern world. He had long since exhausted his local library. Now a major London library kept him supplied with endless reading materials.

The two orders of reality (and there are still *two* in Sankara's structure, because Sankara was categorically *not* a straight-forward monist) are believed to be linked - though the link cannot be too tangible nor secure or it would fetter Brahman to the created cosmos. This would either make the world as unchanging and perfect as its creator; or all the imperfections of the relative world would become shortcomings of Brahman.

The way out was for a link which would not allow for perfect two-way communication between the two orders, a link that would be accessible from Brahman's side, but inaccessible from the other. That link is Isvara, whose being is conceived as both fully divine and fully human - he is a God-Man in whom the two realities are ephemerally linked.

'It is precisely here that we find the place of Isvara as well as one of the functions of Christ, in spite of all the differences which can be found between them,' Mahesh discovered in Panikkar's book *The Unknown Christ of Hinduism.*

This, Mahesh realised, was an excellent solution to the problems of absolute dualism - that if almighty God and the physical world were equally real, then the world could get along perfectly happily without God. For holy God truly to be active in human history, he could not be totally separate from the world, there would have to be some transitory link; one that is 'real' from his side, but which cannot be detected or used from the world's side.

From Advaita Vedanta, Mahesh could see it as intellectually necessary - if one is to believe in a separate God at all - to also believe in a God-Man, Isvara, as a mediator between God and the created world, and without whom the sovereign God can never be perceived or known.

This is true of Christianity and Hinduism alike. The Upanishads and the more recent *Puranas* (composed approx 300-1100 AD) addressed themselves, in part, to analysing the nature of the divine and attempting to define the relationship between Brahman and Isvara. Christians have come to see the relationship as being one of father and son, though theologians argue that this relationship is purely *positional*; father and son are the same, in essence.

A picture begans to emerge for Mahesh:

i) *Nirguna brahman* (literally 'God without attributes' though actually possessing every attribute, none of them differentiated from any other) is only perceivable by us lowly inhabitants of the created order as *Saguna Brahman* (aka 'God with attributes' or Isvara). This is a crucial distinction.

ii) God's creative power, which sustains the universe in existence, acts as a 'veil' preventing us from perceiving almighty God as he really is - limitless, all-wise, pure consciousness, possessing every attribute which we can conceive and many more that we would find inconceivable.

iii) Instead we relate to him only in the limited way we are capable of, in the person of Isvara, who embodies only those functions which are comprehensible to our limited human minds. God is never truly limited; he only allows himself to be perceived that way, as Isvara, so that we might come to know him in a personal way.

Rival Views

Once it is properly comprehended, the difficulties for Muslims, Christians and Jews lie less with Sankara's radical philosophy than with his reactionary theology...

Like many others, Sankara personally believed that Krishna and Isvara were one. In the sectarian Hinduism of Sankara's day, various forms of the deity were each considered supreme by their respective followers, and Sankara's religious sect followed Krishna.

In contrast to Sankara, an eminent eleventh century philosopher of the *visishtadvaita* school named Ramanuja saw the world as completely real, and Vishnu (rather than Siva or Krishna) as encompassing all the roles of Isvara. His philosophy - which we will explore in the next chapter - is less popular than that of Sankara, yet it probably interfaces better with western views.

In one of the pure monist systems, *Kashmir Saivism*, creation is seen simply as the self-projection of universal consciousness or mind which is essentially free, but which has the choice to limit itself by conjouring itself into other objects or entities which can then be reabsorbed. Through ignorance, error or *maya*, these separate objects or entities which owe their existence to consciousness appear to be distinct from it. Omnipotence is lost because of the limiting, and omniscience because of the separation.

In other words, this heretical system states that we are all part of God, but are ignorant of the fact because we have become trapped in matter. *It is this 'extreme' position within Hinduism - which has been taken up more recently by many western cults, particularly scientology and the New Age movement - which forms the basis of much misunderstanding about Hinduism and monism on the part of westerners.*

Of all the founders of religions, L. Ron Hubbard is probably uniquely motivated in founding a faith purely for the tax advantages it confers! Originally a writer of science fiction, many of the elements which go to make a "ripping good yarn" have found their way into the faith of which he became high priest and messiah. In 1950, Hubbard published *Dianetics: The Modern Science of Mental Health,* his psychotherapeutic answer to the world's ills. Hubbard later added a few bits of Hindu mysticism to Dianetics, and served it re-heated as the religion of *Scientology*.

The basic beliefs of this 'new' faith were that mankind is descended from a race of uncreated, omnipotent gods, called *Thetans*. When the Thetans set aside their powers to incarnate within the Material-Energy-Space-Time (MEST) world of Earth, they gradually evolved through reincarnation until they reached the point when they could no longer remember that they were omnipotent beings. Scientology is said to remove the mental blocks, or *engrams*, acquired in past lives which prevent them from realising their Thetan selves and awakening their true personalities and achieving total control over MEST.

It's a bit like a science fiction story, really; one based on *Kashmir Saivism's* claim - that maya deludes all others into thinking that they are different from God when they are actually identical with him - but updated for modern western consumption.

Sankara proposed that *maya* is sustained by *avidya,* or ignorance; yet he fought shy of being too specific about how he perceived this ignorance. For him, it was ineffable, and any description was too limiting. Yet he allowed that the worship of true divinity should culminate in knowledge, *jnana,* which could bring liberation and release from *maya.*

Hubbard claimed that a form of psychotherapy could achieve the same results. At one time, Scientology could claim the active support of five million people world-wide, including hundreds of thousands of committed members - 50,000 in the UK alone. There are several other monist cults which appear to hold the same attraction, such as Silva Mind Control, EST, Lifespring, and Unity.

Silva Mind Control is the brainchild of Jose Silva, whose studies of the mind began with hypnotism and led on to the development of techniques which - he says - will enable his pupils to do anything they wish. In practice, his teaching has much in common with the Raja yoga and Transcendental Meditation which we will encounter later in **Karma 'n' Chips.**

Werner Erhard mixes Scientology with large doses of Nihilism and Zen Buddhism to produce Erhard Seminar Training (EST) - now known as *The Forum* - a set of techniques claimed to produce a state of human perfection, like "gods who have created their own world."

Unity School of Christianity encourages the same kind of positive thinking, apparently within a more orthodox theological framework. But appearances can be deceptive, and there is little in *Unity* that Christ would recognise as stemming from his own teachings. Pantheistic philosophy, a Hindu belief in reincarnation, and a view that redemption is not necessary because evil and sin do not exist, are veiled by an emphasis on love and positive emotions.

These western cults are all the illegitimate offspring of

unorthodox forms of Hindu philosophy which have little to do with true Asian spirituality.

The Vedas Say...

In theory, orthodox Hindu philosophy is based upon the Vedas, just as orthodox Christian thought depends upon the Bible for its foundation. Mahesh had never even heard of the Rig Veda until he had begun his quest for the answers to his son's questions!

Discovering the rich background to his family's faith was fascinating, and Mahesh began to read further and deeper, absorbed by what these two sets of holy scriptures had to say about the origin and nature of the world. He felt it important to read the Bible alongside the Hindu scriptures, as it was a book which has influenced so much of western thought, and he needed answers which were relevant to life in the west.

(Readers who are finding this chapter 'heavy going' might like to skip a few pages to the section headed 'Real Maya'.)

In the Vedas, Mahesh met some of the older gods who have an important bearing on the understanding of the universe, but about whom the average Hindu knows very little - though Hindu priests may be familiar with them.

By the end of the Vedic period, the concept of a creator God - Prajapati - had developed. (The name *Prajapati* eventually changed to the name *Brahma* during the Brahminic period.) Mahesh was puzzled at first by the bewildering myriad of other gods with names like *Indra, Brhaspati and Visvakarman;* but it's likely that all are basically the same god with different names to describe different aspects and functions. As these functions evolved within the development of Hindu theology, so the names changed, think some scholars. Other scholars believe that these were simply different names given to the one creator God by different groups of tribes at different times. We'll probably never know the true explanation.

Vayu the wind god is described as 'one half of Prajapati', who is said to *become* Vayu 'when he has been relaxed and become breath'. Elsewhere, Vayu is called 'the body of Prajapati'. Vayu is said to have been created by Brahma, but is on an equal footing with him; he certainly seemed to have been too important to be simply a different name of Prajapati. Mahesh made a note that Prajapati and Vayu appeared to be the two names worth keeping an eye on as he read further...

Prajapati tends not to be numbered with the myriad other gods and devas, as though he were apart and above them. It appears that Prajapati may be an early name for *Saguna Brahman*, or Isvara, through whom the universe was created, with the participation of Vayu, Mahesh thought.

Prajapati and Purusa

One of the other names of Prajapati is *Purusa*, representing the creator God in the role of the 'supreme cosmic person', sometimes simply called the 'Man'. We could say that the creator God was also the 'Man', or that the world was created by the God-Man...

This 'Man' is a sacrifice, and the past and future are part of him. There is no equal for him, and nothing was born before him, because he is the originator of all. The sage Narayana was the first to postulate that the 'universal basic principle' has the form of a Man; and for him, the term 'Man' was not to be understood in the primal sense as someone with a human body, but in a metaphysical way.

Mahesh began to dip into more of the Hindu creation mythology:

- The *Aitareya Brahmana*: 'Prajapati entertained the desire: "Let me procreate and multiply". He practiced penance and created the earth, the aerial regions and the heaven.' This is similar to the opening of *Genesis*, the first book of the *Holy Bible:* 'In the beginning, God created the heavens and the earth. Now the earth was formless and empty, darkness was over the surface of the deep, and the Spirit of God was moving over the waters. And God said, "Let there be light," and there was light.'

- *The Taittiriya Brahmana* and the *Tandya Brahmana* closely parallels this opening: 'All this was water. From it Prajapati created the earth, the aerial regions and heaven... He destroyed his body and created day, night, twilight and moonlight'; 'In the beginning all this was only Prajapati. There was neither day nor night. He had to crawl in utter darkness. He willed it, he performed the sacrifice, and the day dawned.' The sacrifice referred to was considered to have been a self-sacrifice, according to the priestly writings, the *Brahmanas*.

Gonda explains: 'The creator of the universe is here conceived as the self-limitation of a transcendent person who, without a name or identification, represents Ultimate Reality, manifests himself in the realm of our experience.' The cosmic result of Purusa/Prajapati's sacrifice was first the sacred verbal power (known as the mantra *Om*) and then the various components of creation, including gods and humans.

A constant theme of the Vedic discourses was the human necessity of repeating the example of the primordial event, symbolically reproducing all that it represents. We will return to this subject in a later chapter.

The Bible Says...

In John's Gospel, the 'sacred verbal power' is called the Word, and the Word is Jesus Christ: 'In the beginning was the Word, and the Word was with God, and the Word was God. He was with God in the beginning. Through him all things were made; without him nothing was made that has been made. In him was life, and that life was the light of men. The light shines in the darkness, but the darkness has not understood it.' (John 1:1-5)

Maybe when *nirguna brahman* determined to bring the universe into being, by his creative power (aka his *maya*) God spoke out the word *Om,* limiting himself to being *Saguna Brahman* (aka Prajapati, Purusa, the God-Man) the only begotten Son, though of course he remained *nirguna brahman* as well, two beings locked into the same Godhead.

Denying himself his full range of attributes would certainly constitute self-sacrifice. The act of becoming limited was perhaps the selfsame act of creation which brought the universe into being.

The Rig Veda, too, knows of the 'Word' (*Vac*, in Sanskrit) taking on the role of the supreme principle and ground of the universe; the idea is not exclusive to Christianity, and indeed predates Christianity by many hundreds of years. (Most Asian Christians are wary of the identification of Christ with the word *Om* - not necessarily because of theological difficulties, but because culturally they associate the turgid chanting of *Om* with some of the more superstitious aspects of Hindu spiritual practice. Vac is a more neutral word.)

With the Word came the breath, or wind, Vayu, who could perhaps provisonally be identified with the Holy Spirit, the third person of the trinity. It is said to be through the Spirit and the Word that the unformed universe was shaped and ordered. This tentative scenario is almost equally compatible with both Hinduism and Christianity, and certainly sufficiently full of similarities and parallels to be of great interest to Hindu and Christian alike.

Jesus, the Word, 'is the image of the invisible God, the firstborn over all creation. For by him all things were created: things in heaven and on earth, visible and invisible, whether thrones or powers or rulers or authorities; all things were created by him and for him. He is before all things, and in him all things hold together.' (*Colossians 1:15,16*)

The first twenty-five verses of the first chapter of the Judaeo-Christian book of scripture called *Genesis*, describe how God created the world, light, the sky, dry land, vegetation and animals. These acts of creation by *Purusa* or the Word are closely paralleled in the *Mundaka Upanishad*: 'Splendid and without form is this Purusa, without and within, unborn without life breath and without mind, higher than the supreme element. From him are born life, breath and mind, all the sense organs, also space, air, light, water and earth, the support of all.' (The *Mundaka Upanishad* is of more recent origin than the Genesis account)

Then comes the creation of Man, following a conversation between the members of the triune Godhead: 'Then God said, "Let us make man in our image, in our likeness, and let them rule over the fish of the sea and the birds of the air, over the livestock, over all the earth, and over all the creatures that move along the ground." So God created man in his own image, in the image of God he created him; male and female he created them.' (*Genesis 1:26,27*)

'And the Lord God formed man from the dust of the ground and breathed into his nostrils the breath of life, and man became a living being,' (*Genesis 2:7*)

We are part of the created order from whose particles our bodies are formed, but we receive life from God's indwelling Spirit, Christians believe. Perhaps we can say that human *minds* have independent existence, though like all existence these are sustained by God, using Ramanuja's philosophical reasoning. But the breath or spirit that gives us life is different, it is a part of God, breathed into the first humans and passed on to all their offspring. It is the breath that makes us 'living souls' or sentient beings. The living soul is God's image within us.

Synthesis

The time eventually comes to pull all the strands together and to see what sort of tapestry emerges. Is it possible to flesh out the glimpses of truth in the Hindu sacred books with Christian insights? Can we reconcile authentic revelations of God that are present within the Bible with Hindu philosophies and thought forms, without doing an injustice to either?

For Mahesh, a tentative scenario began to emerge:

i) God, whom we will call *nirguna brahman* (possessing every quality in undifferentiated form, and without any of the limitation through which character and personality are formulated) dwells outside the limits of time.

ii) Time itself is part of his creation. Though God allows himself to dwell there too, he is not *part* of time. God dwells both inside and outside of the space-time continuum, much as an author can be a character in a story he is writing, and can remain himself in both contexts.

iii) When allowing the fullness of his divinity to reside within space-time, he does not permit the whole of his omnipotence and omniscience to reside there - perhaps because of the danger of contamination by unpure souls; partly to prevent the dire consequences if such souls gained access to omnipotence and omniscience; and partly, perhaps, because the naked face of unbridled divinity would be too awesome for people to comprehend.

iv) The act of limiting his attributes might itself have been the prime cause that brought space-time itself into existence, almost as the cage into which he was voluntarily limiting himself. In surpressing many of the attributes he possesses and entering inside time, a differentiated personality emerges replete with all the virtues God chooses, such as the qualities of truth, compassion and love. This would be God *with* attributes - *Saguna Brahman*. This is a personality which can be understood and related to by people within the created order, while the supra-personality of the unlimited Brahman would be totally alien and incomprehensible.

v) *Saguna Brahman,* or Manifest God constitutes a different 'person' sharing the same essential being as *nirguna brahman*, but operating in time rather than eternity. The two would be like father and son. The differentiated personality would be the personal God who can perhaps be called Isvara, or Christ, God's living Word - depending on the liberality of your theological and philosophical tastes! He came to reveal the character of God as Father, and the essence of God's being as the Trinity of Persons, Christians maintain.

vi) This personal God that *nirguna brahman* begat into time would also be called *Purusa*, the Cosmic Man of Hindu myth whose original sacrifice (in being separated from *nirguna brahman*) brought the world into existence: 'By faith we understand that the universe was formed at God's command, so that what is seen was not made out of what was visible.' (*Hebrews 11:3*)

vii) Once the universe was created and sustained by the self-sacrifice of the God-Man - the prototype of a later self-immolation while incarnated on earth as Jesus Christ - the absolute and abstract *nirguna brahman* (God the Father) could become active within it, because he remained one in being with the Cosmic Man *Saguna Brahman* (God the Son).

iix) *Nirguna brahman* when operating *inside* the created order - and thus working in time rather than eternity - might provisonally constitute a third person different from either '*nirguna brahman* operating *outside* the created order', or from '*Saguna Brahman* working within time'. *Nirguna brahman*, when breathed into creation to influence and shape its form, might perhaps be perceived as God's breath or wind (God the Holy Spirit); Vayu in Hindu mythology.

ix) Because one thing that God cannot do is to deny himself, he still exists in eternity as *nirguna brahman*. As such, he stays wholly sovereign and aloof, in holiness and sanctity, the first person of God, remaining - unlike the other two persons who together share in the Godhead - unimaginable and unknowable, more distant than any conception of divinity found within Hinduism. Mortals cannot 'see' the immortal and infinite *nirguna brahman* because two states of being are incompatible: humans are *inside* space-time and *nirguna brahman* is *outside* it. He is wholly distant from the created order, yet two persons who are co-equal with him reside within the created order.

x) He is linked to the world only through himself, and thus can only be known through himself in the person of the God-Man (aka Isvara). It was a truism when Jesus said, 'I am the way and the truth and the life. No one comes to the Father except through me. If you really knew me, you would know my father as well.' (*John 14:6,7*)

When Jesus prays to God, the conversation between two co-eternal members of the Godhead is thus: 'I have brought you glory on earth by completing the work you gave me to do. And now, Father, glorify me in your presence with the glory I had with you before the world began,' (*John 17:4,5*)

(Christians may be concerned or worried about this tentative approach, but it is simply a way of helping some people to come to grips with biblical concepts by putting them in 'Asian clothing'.)

Real Maya

It had been a difficult 'slog' - no wonder people get confused about whether God is personal or impersonal! - but Mahesh was pleased that he had persevered and could now begin to answer his son's questions with more confidence.

Clearly, he would need to put off any detailed explanation until the young lad was much older; for now, he could simply sit his son on his knee and say honestly, 'I don't know very much about it all, but I believe that God made the world and everything in it, and that He is a unique being worshipped by Christians and Hindus alike.' That was not something which Mahesh Patel had expected to find. He would feel much more comfortable in his daily life knowing that Christians were not such a strange and different species from himself after all!

Mahesh found it difficult to explain his discoveries to his Asian friends and relations, however, because of all their preconceptions. From the lay person's viewpoint, the word *maya* is still used in many Hindu (and Sikh) worship songs to mean that the world is *kuri*, or false; that we live in a phantom universe. Sankara's philosophy has been so influential, but so misunderstood, that the mistaken interpretations of previous generations have become perpetuated as 'truth', however paradoxical the implications might be:

> *Standing there upon the stair,*
> *I saw a man who wasn't there.*
> *He wasn't there again today,*
> *I really wish he'd go away!*

'Don't believe the world is real, don't trust it,' many Asians state. 'Be as detached as possible from your possessions, your wife, your children,' they say - though detachment is a Buddhist concept, not a Hindu idea. The media has become the message, and many

Asian songs are a message of detachment, making an illusory and intangible world a powerful concept in the typical Asian mind, even though the belief is incorrect. Just because many people believe something to be true doesn't make it correct. In ancient times, people believed that the world was flat - but their belief didn't make it true!

Many feel that their religion must be a fixed constant - like the speed of light, it can never change. Because they believe that people can't alter their beliefs, when someone does, they pretend it never happened - often by dismissing the person who did it. Any transformation is anathema, treated as unreal, and greeted with intolerance. Change your faith and you will be persecuted for it, out of blind fear of the social repercussions such a 'disgrace' might bring into the happy Asian home. (Hindus are, of course, often inconsistent in their beliefs. If the world *is* really illusion, then the family member's 'conversion' isn't real either!)

Paradoxically, illusion has become a reality in many Indian houses, because the notion of living in an ethereal world can expediently cover a multitude of intolerant attitudes, and excuse shabby behaviour! *A very familiar concept, it is used to explain away many unequal aspects of life.* Great wealth, for example: If you have it, you can shrug off any blame for the way in which it was acquired by saying 'it's all illusion'. The idea is also used in slums as an excuse for not trying to better oneself. This view of maya often lends itself to superstitious fatalism, too. 'I could get a better life, even in an unreal state, but it's all written anyway, isn't it?'

It is used wrongly as an excuse for perpetuating the status quo, when in fact, maya is God's creation - filled with meaning and purpose, pregnant with limitless capability and potential for change.

Science Says...

Sharma, in *A Hindu Perspective on the Philosophy of Religion*, says 'any material element which is not capable of division constitutes an ultimate. Thus, those constituents of matter which are infinitesimally small, for example atoms, or those which are infinitely large, space for example, are ultimates. It is out of these that God fashions the universe...'

This is the view of some schools of Hindu thought, where God is seen as ordering matter that is already there, rather than forming it himself. In Christianity, this concept fits well with some interpretations of *Genesis 1:2*, which read 'the earth was formless and empty' as referring to the debris of some previous creative event.

Scientists believe that the universe began about twenty-five billion years ago. Energy exploded outwards from a single point, not into a pre-existing space-time continiuum, but creating space and time as it went. As the temperature of the original inferno cooled, atomic nuclei and atoms formed, and were drawn together into clouds of dust from which the stars formed.

One enigmatic question which science is unable to answer is '*Why* did the universe come into existence?' What triggered that titanic eruption of space-time, matter and energy? The most popular scientific theories speak of a 'quantum fluctuation' - a 'momentary unevenness in the smooth undifferentiated potential' - that allowed a few pairs of particles to come into spontaneous existence, followed by a cascade that pushed the phenomenon beyond the point of no return. Once started, the process was unstoppable. But what caused it to start? It's a question which science cannot answer, and which properly still remains within the esoteric providence of religion.

Though the earth upon which we stand is firm beneath our feet, if we were to set out into space in a random direction, the universe is so void of matter that we might travel for a million light years without ever encountering any solid matter larger than a few molecules of dust.

Going inwards instead of outwards, we discover that the ground is actually made of molecules, which are in turn made of hollow atoms. Atoms are composed of electrons rotating around a central core, but consist almost entirely of empty space. The diameter of an atom is about a hundred millionth of a centimeter, and its nucleus is so small that even if the atom were blown up to the size of a room, we could not see it with the unaided eye. Blow up the atom to the size of the dome of St Peter's cathedral in Rome, and the nucleus will be about the size of a grain of salt.

When Sankara says that the physical universe is *close to being* an illusion, it is clear to see that - through God's eyes - with such an absence of solid matter, it barely exists. The philosopher was remarkably accurate with his views given more than a millenium before modern science showed them to be accurate!

Scientific theory suggest that the physical universe is composed of equal quantities of matter and anti-matter. Scientists are unable to ascertain where all the anti-matter is to be found, but if it reacted with ordinary matter each type of matter would instantly annihilate the other. If this is so, the universe is sustained in existence only because the two types of matter are 'somehow' kept apart. Perhaps our contined existence really is due to God's sustaining power, his **true** *maya*.

The Vedas say that the universe exhibits a cyclic pattern of successive destruction and restoration. Scientists say that if the gravitational attraction of all the matter in the cosmos is stronger than the force with which the universe is exploding outwards, the universe's expansion will begin to slow, and eventually creation will contract back onto itself in a cataclysmic implosion. Then, perhaps the whole thing will start over again. Scientific estimates of the total gravitational mass of the universe are still very rough, but current estimates suggest that the universe is close to the critical mass that would eventually cause contraction to occur.

Orphans of the Universe?

Though science has done much to support religious views, it has also contributed much to the erosion of human dignity. When a person feels that they are but a small drop in a large ocean, with no importance, living a life that can have no consequence in such a vast universe, it can be bitterly alienating.

The misunderstanding that many have of *maya*, believing it to mean that the universe is an ethereal phantom, has had dire consequences on the Hindu social order. The voice of Everyman cries out: 'If everything is so rarified that the whole of creation is little more than a hallucination, it doesn't matter what pain I am going through.'

Maya misunderstood to mean 'illusion' is a strand of religious thought that, permeating daily living, has held India back from its rightful position on the world's stage. People in shanty towns put up with their lot because they are led to understand that it somehow isn't real anyway. Fatalism and superstition have run rampant amongst Asian communities in the east and west alike; and a morbid belief in destiny - 'it is written' so I have no control over it - leads them to believe that they can have no control over their own lives:

'If God is so large and I am so small, what is the point

of living?'

To claim that *maya* is fantasy and deception, instead of God's power in creation, is a beguiling attempt to substitute for God. Rather than submitting to his grace, love and authority, people say, 'well, nothing really exists anyway', and seek any convenient alternative explanation to the truth.

'In my family, it was common to have teaching on *maya* and the nebulous nature of existence,' remembers one ordinary British Asian. 'Hindu priests would frequently castigate Asian businessmen at the *mandir* or temple for making money; at home, I would hear the same businessmen say to one another, "If it's all unreal, why do we bother to pay the priests? They say it's all illusion, but then they come with their bill at the end of the day!"'

An illusion? When God seems to have created an enormous, complex and subtly balanced universe?

Two chapters ago, we set out to explore basic beliefs about Man, God and the Universe. It's now time to backtrack from the awesome majesty of God and the immenseness of the created order, to explore the role of the individual within it. Questions like 'Is there a divine plan?''How can I relate to God?'and 'What is God like?' are all very well; but at the end of the day, the small voice in each of our hearts still cries out, like a hurt and frightened child, the age-old question *'Who am I?'*

The time has come to explore the answers to that question.

'There is one spectacle grander than the sea;
there is one spectacle grander than the sky,
that is the interior of the soul.'
Victor Hugo

CHAPTER

4

ATMAN: *Can you see the real 'me'?*

'Atman' looks as though it ought to be the name of a costumed super-hero; a caped crusader or a man of steel, leaping tall buildings with a single bound!

The truth is perhaps stranger - and much more incredible - than fiction.

Atman (actually pronounced 'ahtmah') together with *Brahman*, are the two central 'characters' who dominate the teaching of the Upanishads. They are the Self and the Ultimate; a potent combination, and - like all good super heroes, *atman* is the alter ego or 'secret identity' of the Brahman. Or so many Hindus believe.

Atman is the 'essence of sentience'; it is 'utter consciousness', some say. But what do they mean? The closest western equivalent might be the human spirit or soul, but that too can be misleading. *It is perhaps a synonym for the unfathomable!*

About *atman*, Hindu philosophy says that only one reply is possible: *Neti, Neti* (literally 'not this, not this') For every possible definition, one is compelled to say that 'it doesn't apply'. *Atman* is totally 'other'. It does not undergo birth or death, as graphically described in the *Bhagavad Gita*: 'Unborn, eternal, everlasting, ancient, it is not killed when the body is killed.'

However we attempt to define it, the *atman*'s presence within us at least means that humans are more than just a physical body. As former-Beatle George Harrison says, 'This impermanent body, a bag of bones and flesh, is mistaken for our true self,' when it's not. The *atman* concept at the very least is a denial of secular materialism - the notion that the physical world is all that exists. The *Gita* affirms that the body is mortal while *atman*, the divine spark in man, is immortal, eternal and all-pervading. As long as *atman* and body are together, human activity is natural and inevitable.

Some western scholars, as well as some Hindus, think that *atman* and *Brahman* are absolutely identical. The Upanishads generally follow one of two distinct paths. The first begins with the outside world and reduces it to one essence. The other commences with a person's subjective consciousness and discovers within its depths, the objective source of everything. The conclusion of both journeys ends in the realisation of *Brahman*. The power that steers the stars is small enough to fit inside a person.

'Finally the realisation dawns that the immanent *atman* is identical with the transcendental *Brahman*: *atman* is *Brahman*,' says Klostermaier. Well, that might be the case if you go along with Sankara's interpretation, but one can imagine Sankara's critics being a mite put out by such a fait accompli!

If the *atman* is the real 'me', then to say that '*atman* and *Brahman* are one' sounds like saying 'we are all God' - the basic consequence of monism. The idea that the supreme being is identical with the personal spirit, the real 'me', which dwells within each of us - *like the notions that Hinduism is polytheistic, monist, proposes an impersonal deity, and advocates an illusory universe* - is not the idea it cracks up to be!

'We Are All *Brahman*'?

Like those other 'misunderstandings', the idea that *atman* and the real 'me' are completely as one, is a misinterpretation of what the Upanishads and their chief interpreters actually say...

'In many passages *atman* means not the individual soul but "the soul of All" and is therefore merely another word for Brahman. To identify the two in this sense is pure tautology,' Professor Zaehner insists. *Atman* is not necessarily the real 'me'.

One of the most famous verses in the Hindu sacred books says: 'Know the *atman* to be sitting in the chariot, the body to be the chariot, the intellect the charioteer, and the mind the horses.' *(Mundaka Upanishad II.II)* If the *atman* is not our intellect or our mind, then how is it in any way the person that I call 'myself'?

Atman is technically 'the grammatic form of the third-person reflexive personal pronoun' in Sanskrit. It can mean the body, or anything one considers to be a part of oneself, depending on the context; but, deriving from the *third person* pronoun, it does not simply mean 'me' or 'I' in the everyday sense. *Atman* is *not* simply the personal soul, that aspect of ourselves which we might consider to be the real 'me'.

The *atman* is an 'it' or a 'he', not a 'me'!

There is general agreement that the individual soul within us all starts in a state of purity, but becomes contaminated or re-purified depending on actions performed in life. However, if this individual soul is the *atman* and *atman* is God, then it would mean that human actions were contaminating the eternal God. Something is badly wrong there, somewhere.

Just as the value of your car, when you come to sell it, will depend on how well you have driven it, serviced it and generally cared for it, so - in Hinduism and Christianity alike - the condition of the frail human spirit or soul is affected by actions performed in life. The real 'me' is a long way from being God!

Its fate and its state can also be affected after departing this life, through strange rituals that are performed by the deceased's relatives, according to Hindus. Its journey in the afterlife is not forgotten, and Hindus often pay priests highly to perform sacrifices to 'ease the soul's passage', particularly at funerals and at the anniversary of death. In some cases, the bereaved have money literally snatched from their hands by cruel charlatans who claim that they can 'help the departed soul'.

There used to be a similar concept in Roman Catholicism, whereby relatives could help the spirits of the departed by paying for a special Mass to be held, making a pilgrimage, or buying special 'dispensations'. This bizarre sale of 'indulgences' as they were known, went on for several centuries before a German theologian named Martin Luther looked at what the religious texts actually said, and discovered that there was no scriptural basis for the practice!

This discovery, and the internal struggles within the Church led to the Reformation, during the sixteenth century. Such a reformation, whereby practice is brought into line with scripture has never occurred in Hinduism. Perhaps that needs to happen in the near future...

'That Thou Art'?

We've seen that 'I' am not the *atman* - the *atman* is not the real 'me'. 'So who, or what, *is* the real me?' cries the human heart in its deepest moments of dispair. 'Am I just a clockwork being, wound up when I leave the womb, and left to wind down? I have my family and my job, but what purpose or meaning has my life really got?

'What dignity can I have if I'm no more than a few fistfuls of chemicals, driven by basic animal instincts? Why do I suffer so much?' These are the problems and these the cries of all humanity, regardless of colour or creed.

Why?

'I have been noticing from my childhood that my parents, my relatives and most of my acquaintances always expect gods or goddesses to offer them a ready-made solution whenever they have problems, ' says Arabinda Dey in his soul-searching autobiography *I Confess*. 'When I was growing up, I started wondering whether our gods and godesses were so greedy that they would do anything for us if we offered them some fruits, flowers and sweets. "Well, has anyone ever seen these goddesses," I used to wonder... [I always received] the same obscurist answer, "You cannot meet them. They are much above you."

'I started thinking: "There must be some supreme guardian of this world and the cosmos. And that guardian cannot be harsh and unsympathetic. And the way to Him may not be full of roses, but it is not full of thorns either." I started looking at God's exquisite creations all around. I asked myself, "Is there no one who can show me the way to the creator of all these things?" ' Perhaps there *is* such a one...

Let's come back to the notion of the *atman*. We've discovered that *atman* is not the same as the personal self - the person we each call 'me' - but perhaps *atman* may still be *Brahman*. We are not, of ourselves, God; but do we have God *within* us? Perhaps we can't find the true ruler and guardian of the cosmos because we've been looking in the wrong place; we've been looking outwards instead of inwards. Being a living temple in which God dwells would certainly give us a useful purpose, and a vital connection with the infinite divine. Let's look at that possibility.

Is *atman* perhaps a synonym for that mystical part of the divine nature that was first conferred upon humanity when God breathed into the first man? That which you and I *consider* to be 'the real me' might be just our minds or souls. 'Our' *atman* - our essential spiritual part - may simply be an attribute that we are loaned until the one to whom it rightly belongs, *Brahman*, requires its return.

The *Chandogya Upanishad* says: 'The *atman* who is free from all evil, free from old age, free from death, free from worry, free from hunger and thirst... he should be sought, him one must strive to understand. One who has found the *atman* and understands him attains all worlds and the fulfillment of all desires.'

Far from likening the *atman* to the personal self, this *sruti* or Hindu scripture, seems to imply that *atman* is *not* our own essential self. Instead, it is something (or someone) that we desperately need to find and know. That 'finding' may need to take place at an internal level, deep within each of us, but the phrasing hardly implies that the finding depends upon any kind of 'self realization'.

The *Atharva Veda* says that 'who knows the *atman* of man knows the highest Lord,' *(10.7.17)* apparently viewing *atman* as synonymous - not with Man - but with God. The *Mundaka Upanishad* explains how *Brahman* is said to have entered into all created things, but that the created order is not all part of *Brahman*.

At every step, atman seems more and more to be an attribute of God residing in man, but of a wholly different nature, rather than anything we would recognise as our own characters or personality.

'The Upanishads do not present a fully developed theological system, they offer experiences and visions. The Upanishadic *atman* is not simply and unequivocally identical with *Brahman* under all circumstances, only in *turiya*, the real consciousness of the Upanishads, which is not easily accessible,' confirms Klostermaier. *Atman* and *Brahman* are only identical when both are stripped of all qualities - so for our own *atman* to become *brahman* would lead to the extinction of the qualities of our individual personality and be the equivalent of cosmic suicide!

What more do the Hindu religious texts have to say? The *Shvetashvatara* (VI.9,11) says the *atman* 'is without parts, action, change, defect, virtue and vice; it is the supreme bridge leading to immortality; and it is like fire that has burnt out its fuel... The one God, hidden in all things, all-pervading, the Inner Soul of all, the overseer of all deeds, in all things abiding, the witness, the sole thinker, devoid of qualities.' Devoid of qualities is hardly a description that could apply to an individual like you or me; it sounds sublimely like *nirguna brahman*...

Some scholars believe that the word *atman* was first used to denote the breath (*prana*) or wind (*vayu*). It is also conceived as pervading the physical universe. Various deities are called *atman*. Vayu, of course is a Hindu deity whom we have tentatively compared with the Holy Spirit of the Bible. The *atman* is sometimes call 'The Self' but only in the sense that 'The Self' is another Hindu name for God, much as God's name in Judaeo-

Christian tradition is given as 'I am'.

Though, as we said in the Introduction, theology cannot easily be gleaned from Hindu scriptures in quite the compliant manner that the Bible affords us clear revelation, a rough Hindu theology does eventually emerge from scrutiny of the texts.

The most straight forward interpretation is that God's spirit lives within each of us, like an esteemed house guest, having been breathed into us by God (atman derives from a root word meaning 'to breathe') and that each of us can perceive it only by seeing the world and ourselves in a totally new way.

Sankara's *Atman*

Atman is the very heart of divinity. We need to transcend our normal worldly outlook and find God within us, if we are to perceive our true value and worth. How can this be done?

The *Mundaka Upanishad* answers the question succinctly, after first explaining how it *cannot* be acheived: not by *pravachana* (discussion or instruction), nor by *medha* (intellectual capacity), nor by *bahu sruti* (hearing the sacred texts). *Atman* reveals its form (*tanu*) only to the person that it chooses. *No possible ambiguity is left in the text by the grammatical construction: it is the atman itself that does the choosing, and no human effort can ensure its attainment.*

That seems quite straight forward: we don't discover the *atman*, the *atman* finds us. 'But not so for Sankara. By one of those extraordinary distortions of grammar and lexicon which is usual for him, he interprets the passage to mean that the *atman* is attainable by a man if he is eager enough in seeking knowledge,' criticises Nirad Chaudhuri in his 1977 book, *Hinduism*. Yet this is a break with the entire Upanishadic tradition of mysticism. *Sankara's religious views at this point cease to be authentically Asian or genuinely Hindu in his theology. But he does have philosophical insights which make up for his theological deficiencies:*

Just as Sankara distinguished between *Saguna* and *nirguna* Brahman, he made an important esoteric distinction between two types of *atman*: the *paramatman* (higher self) and the *jivatman* (the individual self). He regretted that the *paramatman* was not recognised as the highest *atman* by all people, but considered that it was indeed God, the Real, the subtle essence behind the *jivatman*, which we might want to call the individual soul. He believed that what the unlearned called real (the *jivatman*) was 'shrouded by ignorance' and consequently misconceived as separate from the supreme *paramatman*. It was out of such a state of ignorance that he graciously sought to lead his student in the quest for the real *paramatman*.

One must make the constant effort to 'remain absorbed' in the *atman* - otherwise God's protective power, his *maya*, will veil the ultimately real, project the unreal, and misdirect the mind to the lower level of reality, warned Sankara. A mind that wanders is an unwise mind. Even the great intellectual himself was prone to such lapses according to one humourous story. The philosopher was humbled when he once ordered an outcaste to stand aside as he walked with his disciples to perform their rituals:

'You ask me to move aside and make way for you,' said the outcaste. 'To whom were your words addressed? To the body? Or to the *atman* which is the same in all? How do such differences as "This is a brahmin, this is an outcaste" arise in non-dual experience?'

Sankara became convinced from this that a man's outlook and not the caste of his birth should determine his status.

Atman and the Bible

Christians reading **Karma'n'Chips** may have spotted something faintly familiar. The concept of the *atman* doing the choosing is similar to the Christian idea that God is not found by man, but that God takes the initiative. To Christianise the Hindu concept, *jivatman* could be the individual's soul, which God seeks to draw to himself in *paramatman*.

As St Paul says: 'When we were still powerless, Christ died for the ungodly... God demonstrates his love for us in this: While we were still sinners, Christ died for us... We know that in all things God works for the good of those who love him, who have been called according to his purpose. For those God foreknew he also predestined to be confirmed to the likeness of his Son, that he might be the firstborn among many brothers. And those he predestined, he also called; those he called, he also justified; those he justified, he also glorified.' *(Romans 5:6,8; 8:28-30)*

In the Jewish *Torah*, too, God says through the prophet Hosea: 'I will call them "my people" who are not my people; and I will call her "my loved one" who is not my loved one. *(Hosea 2:23)*

To paraphrase St Paul: 'Because of his great love for us, Brahman, who is rich in mercy, made us alive with *Isvara* even when we were dead in transgressions - it is by grace you have been saved. And *nirguna brahman* raised us up with *Isvara* and seated us with him in the heavenly realms in *Saguna Brahman*. For it is by grace that you have been saved, through faith - and this is not from yourselves, it is the gift of *Saguna Brahman* - not by works, so that no man can boast. For we are *nirguna brahman*'s workmanship, created in *Isvara* to do good works, which *Brahman* prepared in advance for us to do.' *(From Ephesians 2:4-10)*

With God doing the choosing, the trackless universe may not have to seem such a lonely place after all. If the *atman* were simply our 'higher selves' as Sankara (and many New Agers) propose - or we were ourselves 'divine', but suffering from amnesia like L. Ron Hubbard's 'thetans' - then we would still be left foresaken with only the poor solace of our own dreary company. If we carry our own tiny tin 'god' inside us, as a part of our own poor selves, to be battered and tarnished by our ethical ineptitudes, we are 'up the creek', to use a western metaphor.

Entirely through his grace and owing nothing to ourselves - ready to receive and support our inner nature, then in Christian terms, *atman* is none other than God's Holy Spirit, our true friend in times of trouble, and the one who chooses us! 'Surely you know that you are God's temple and that God's Spirit lives within you!' (*1 Corinthians 3:16*)

What is man?

One day in 1968, Arabinda Dey was going to offer *puja* at a temple in Gauhati, hoping that it would bring him success in a forthcoming job interview. He recalls walking beneath a sky ablaze with colour, his mind filled with disturbing questions about his ancestral faith:

'A man is born. He is brought up properly. He gets educated, does some job or other, earns money, gets married in due course and brings forth children. Then one day, inevitably, comes old age. And, after that, everything ends up in death.

'Then - what is the use of this human life? What is the purpose? How is man greater than the other animals of the world? All the other animals also eat, sleep, get old and die. Where is then the greatness of man? How is man different from the others?'

Three thousand years earlier, a middle-eastern king had no doubts about the answers to those sort of questions:

'O Yahweh, our Lord, how majestic is your name in all the earth!' he cried to *Saguna Brahman*, using the deity's most intimate, personal name. 'When I consider your heavens, the work of your fingers, the moon and the stars, which you have set in place, what is man that you are mindful of him, the son of man that you care for him? You made him a little lower than the heavenly beings and crowned him with glory and honour. You made him ruler over the works of your hands; you put everything under his feet: all flocks and herds, and the beasts of the field, the birds of the air, and the fish of the sea, all that swim the paths of the sea. O Yahweh, our Lord, how majestic is your name in all the earth!' (*Psalm 8:1,3-9*)

King David had no doubts whatsoever about man's significance. In himself, he had no importance whatsoever! King or pauper, there was nothing he could do to gain value for himself. Yet he possessed inestimable honour through being created and loved by God and 'crowned with glory and honour'. When Arabinda Dey discovered this for himself, he became a follower of Jesus Christ...

For King David, the living essence of his being, his *atman*, possessed inestimable value and dignity through being charged with God's power and authority - given freely as an act of unmerited favour, God's grace flowing unchecked. The Christian can say, 'I have value and worth because I am loved by God.' This is a view fervidly shared by many eminent Hindu theologians, including Madhva and Ramanuja:

Ramanuja's *Atman*

Seeing *maya* as 'God's power manifest in creation', the philosopher Ramanuja eruditely agreed with Sankara in considering the created order to be *lila*, or divine play, but he considered personal devotion to be more important than abstruse esoteric knowledge. He argued that the astonishing human soul has *atman* within it - as an *antaryamin*, or 'inner controller', whom he identified with God. But unlike Sankara, he passionately believed each precious soul to be independently real in its own right.

Ramanuja's *Visistadvaita Vedanta* school of thought suggests that, without Brahman's permission, a human soul is powerless to operate; but when a soul does function, the moral responsibility for action always rests with the particular soul that wills it, because Brahman does not interfere with the individual's freedom of choice. This is the only Hindu school that attempts to explain the relationship between God's grace and the deeds of the individual.

Ramanuja persuasively suggested that the sublime Brahman is not a homogeneous entity, but one containing within itself 'elements of plurality' because of which it truly manifests itself in a diversified world. He says 'All this is indeed Brahman!' - not in any pantheistic sense - but meaning that the panoramic cosmos is so permeated with God's Spirit that it has no existence independent of its sublime creator. In Christian terms, Ramanuja - like Sankara - has difficulties in adequately describing both the united Godhead and the persons within it; though, for Ramanuja, God is less remote than for Sankara, and personal dignity is enhanced accordingly.

Klostermaier comments that all-in-all Ramanuja 'can claim to have Hindu tradition on his side and that, on the whole, his interpretation of the Vedas may be fairer than Sankara's.' It seems that Sankara may be the best philosopher, but Ramanuja is the better theologian. His writings return to the premise that God benevolently makes possible a personal relationship with himself:

The Supreme Brahman, 'creates the entire universe out of primal elements controlled by the spiritual souls in material conjunction,' and then of his own accord enters into them as their *antaryamin* or inner controller, writes Ramanuja in his *Vedanta Samgraha*. Like Sankara, he distinguishes between *parmaatman* and *jivatman* - though he declines to use the same names, preferring the roughly equivalent expressions, *antaryamin* and *soul*. When souls realise that an 'ocean of immeasurable and absolute goodness, beauty and love is the principal to which the soul is accessory or subserveant, then the Supreme Brahman who is thus an object of absolute love leads the souls to himself.'

In *The Religion of Ramanuja: A Christian Appraisal*, Devamani comments that 'Ramanuja's theological thought of God and the redemption of the world, probably seem to be quite similar to that of Christian understanding. Ramanuja's theology is generally most helpful and valuable in India as well as in other parts of the world in philosophical and theological teaching of God.' For him, Brahman is a God of grace who seeks to unite man with himself.

Journey into Grace

Is the relationship between God and the individual soul a legalistic connection dependent upon esoteric wisdom and rooted in arcane ritual (Sankara's view), or a bond of love stemming from grace (Ramanuja's view)? In communities across the globe, the outworkings of such heated debate can tear families apart as each side argues that only its own views are authentically Asian.

For Mrs Singh, it was all a terrible nightmare! Her beautiful home in the expatriate Asian community in Nairobi had become the scene of unseemly fighting and squabbling. It was all the fault of her new daughter-in-law, bringing in strange new ideas that were at odds with the religion which her family had always practised.

She and her husband had always been very ritualistic with their temple worship of Siva, and the family guru had always been clear with her and her husband that theirs was the right way to perform religious duties. Now their son's new bride had come with strange ideas of 'grace', stemming from devotion, being a better path to God than gurus or ritual. Why, it all sounded so western, and very *un-Asian!*

In fact, Mrs Singh has nothing to fear from her daughter-in-law. The concept of grace has long been as indigenous to Asian spirituality as offering food to idols, performing *arti*, or chanting *mantras*. It bestows greater nobility upon the individual worshipper than the often demeaning rituals, prostrating oneself before a statue or Siva *lingum*. The different viewpoints have emanated from Asian theologians, and no side can claim an exclusive monopoly on truly Asian spirituality. Such disputes need to be resolved by discussion - not by throwing people out of the family home.

Grace is the central concept of Ramanuja's *vaishnavist* form of Hinduism - the idea of grace, or 'unmerited favour', is by no means confined to Christianity. For *vaishnavism*, redemption is a justification by faith. A devout follower of Ramanuja's tradition can use words borrowed from the Christian tradition without any embarrassment!

According to Srinivasachari, grace that is not caused by human righteousness is like *mulaipal*, mother's breast milk, given freely; while grace that is dependent upon human goodness is like *vilaippal*, purchased milk that is often diluted and adulterated. True grace comes directly from God.

Ramanuja wrote: 'We know from scripture that there is a supreme person whose nature is absolute bliss and goodness, who is the cause of the organisation, sustenation and dissolution of the world, who differs in nature from all other beings, who is all-knowing, who by his mere thought and will accomplish all his purposes, who is an ocean of kindness, as it were, for all who depend on him, whose name is the highest Brahman.' And many Christians say 'Amen' in affirmation of that!

To summarise: For Ramanuja, Brahman is essentially a personal God all along. Ramanuja makes no distinction between Isvara and Brahman; and individual souls, though all objectively real, draw their reality directly from Brahman.

In some respects, theologically, Sankara's view is similar to the Muslim view of the supreme God as a distant and impersonal figure, while Ramanuja is close to the Christian view seeing him as eminently personal and knowable. Paradoxically though, Ramanuja's view that God is indivisibly one, is the Islamic view; while Sankara's view easily allows for persons to exist within the Godhead, an idea closer to the Christian standpoint.

Each is half-right and half-wrong on this basis; though according to a *complete* Christian understanding, Sankara fails to grasp the full implications of a triune God, which makes him the poorer theologian, by Christian standards. Though Ramanuja is unable to conclusively defeat Sankara's theology with a clear knock-out blow, the Upanishads and the Bible are both more on his side, and at the end of the intellectual 'boxing contest' he probably wins on points!

Paths to God

Ramanuja commented on the Bhagavad Gita 4:6 ('Though I am unborn and inexhaustible in my own nature, though I am the Lord of all beings, yet abiding in my own nature, I am born of my own free will') that Lord Krishna was born on earth 'without in the least giving up any of the special qualities of the Supreme Ruler... imperishable, being the Lord of all.' i.e. He is not compelled to assume bodily form because of *karma* or anything else. He does not abandon any of his essential divine nature. *Krishna exemplifies the God-Man.*

Dhavamony summarises the Gita's teaching about Krishna: 'He who realises by knowledge the real meaning of Krishna's life and work by which he protects the good and makes them take refuge in him, such a person after giving up the present body...obtains him only. Through knowledge of Krishna's divine birth and work, all

the sins that stand in the way of resorting to him are destroyed...
Knowledge of the divine incarnation, combined with loving
meditation on God, helps one reach the goal of salvation which
consists of loving union with and surrender to Krishna.' *So
knowing the true and living God-Man is the key to knowing God...*

Though Dhavamony is correct about the Gita's teaching on
Krishna's role and his work with the individual, he is of course
incorrect in assuming that *knowledge* is the key by which Krishna
may be known. Such a position reflects Sankara's view, but not the
views of Ramanuja or Madhva nor the clearest meaning of the
Gita itself.

Krishna could not have been clearer when he said to Arjuna: 'All
those who take refuge in me, whatever their birth, race, sex or
caste, will attain the supreme goal; this realisation can be attained
even by those whom society scorns. Kings and sages too seek their
goal with devotion. Therefore, having been born into this transient
and forlorn world, give all your love to me. Fill your mind with me;
love me; serve me; worship me always. Seeking me in your heart,
you will at last be united with me,' *(Gita 9.32-34)*

No mention here of esoteric knowledge. The clear message is
that Krishna (or the God-Man) is reached by devotion, love, service
and worship! Move over, Sankara; on the basis of this well-known
text, Ramanuja's position and Madhva's stance (which we will see
in the following chapter) are in accordance with both the Vedas
and the Bible:

St Paul says: 'We know that we all possess knowledge.
Knowledge puffs up, but love builds up. The man who thinks he
knows something does not yet know as he ought to know. But the
man who loves God is known by God.' *(1 Corinthians 8:1-3)*

'In the lotus of nine doors (the human body) enveloped in the
three strands there dwells a supernatural being (*yaksha*) possessed
of *atman*; this do those who know Brahman know. Free from desire
it is, wise, immortal, self-existent, delighting in savour, no wise
lacking. Knowing this *atman*, wise and ageless [yet ever] young,
one has no fear of death.' *(Atharva Veda 10.8)*

Here, in the Vedic tradition is clear affirmation that knowledge
comes into the frame of salvation *only* in the sense that it is
necessary to *know personally* the eternal, self-existent God-Man,
whose *atman* sustains the life in our mortal bodies, in order to
begin to acheive the ultimate goal of life, fulfillment of the
sanatana dharma. But *grace* is the prime divine attribute which
allows God to become known to humans.

Only when 'knowing God' leads us on to faith, devotion and love for the supreme God as revealed in the God-Man, is the paramatman, which might be another name for the Holy Spirit, free to lead our own personalities and memories - our souls - with it to the very heart of divinity, to be with God forever. This is the ultimate goal for Christians and Hindus alike.

There is a 'down' side to the coin though, Christians believe. The problem can be put into an Asian context as follows: *When the God-Man is not personally encountered and loved by the individual, the live-sustaining paramatman will still return to Brahman at some point, after our physical death. If the paramatman was never 'known', loved and united with our own personal soul or jivanatman - if we did not accept the God-Man into our life as a personal reality - then our personalities and memories will not be taken to Brahman with the paramatman. We will never 'know' Brahman. The 'real me', the jivatman in each of us, will be lost for all eternity!*

Christ - God's sacred utterance, the living word or God-Man - Christians believe. This simple way of fulfilling the *sanatana dharma* is called the *Gospel*, or the 'good news' which Christ came to bring to Asian and westerner alike. Merely following a family faith will not do the job - the decision is a personal one which must actively be made by each family member of their own volition.

As Dhavamony says, 'man is divine through God's gift of making him share the divine nature which is in no way due to man, and salvation is the restoration of this participation in the divine nature of God in and through Christ to whom man responds and with whom he enters union.' As the *Mundaka Upanishad* has it, the arrow of the *atman* is released from the bow of the mystic syllable Om into the target of the Brahman. *(2.2.4)*

The Avatar

Ramanuja did not conceive God's graciousness merely as an intellectual attribute, the Hindu doctrine of the *avatar* shows God at work in practice, coming to earth to help people in need. The word *avatar* derives from the Sanskrit *avataranam* meaning 'descent'.

Ramanuja's writings refer to four kinds of incarnation:

i) Direct incarnation, where the fullness of the Godhead resides within the physical form from the moment of conception in the mother's womb.

ii) An aspect of God that is less than the fullness entering the soul of a distinguished sage or prophet.

iii) God lending his strength to a mortal temporarily for some good reason.

iv) God entering any form in order to be worshipped.

Only the first kind really does justice to the idea of incarnation being truly 'God in the flesh'. God comes of his own accord, and is not compelled to come. Nor does he lay aside his own essential nature.

The concept of sublime God becoming incarnate is, in origin and development, authentic to the *sanatana dharma* that we know as Hinduism. It is not an outside influence that has been gratuitously grafted on. Belief in divine embodiment was a fresh refinement following the brahminist era, though in the Hindu conception the incarnation or *avatar* is never a 'redeemer' who personally takes on the responsibilities of the human race and rescues it from the consequences of sin. For the Hindu, the incarnation of Brahman is simply to help and guide mankind, and not for any metaphysical rescue mission. This is the only (slight) difference to the Christian conception of incarnation.

Zaehner notes that the word 'Brahman' can be accented in one of two different ways, with an accent on the first 'a' or on the second 'a'. In the first case, the word literally means 'sacred utterance', as we have already discussed. In the second case, it means 'a masculine person *imbued with the power* of the sacred utterance or word' - such a person may be a god, a man or perhaps a God-Man, Brahman-atman, a physical embodiment or *avatar*.

Though many consider that for Sankara, incarnation is virtually an impossibility - because from God's viewpoint, there is no real world in which to be incarnated! - he is again misrepresented here as postulating an ethereal 'phantom' universe which is not truly the case.

Ramanuja maintains that the personification of divinity is an actual truth and that God's incarnation embodies the divine nature in full measure. The incarnation is one of pure goodness to save the virtuous, to redeem the sinner and to punish the wicked.

Ramakrishna (1834-86) regarded Christ as an incarnation like Buddha or Rama, whereby God manifests the perfection of divinity. He can manifest himself in prophets only partially, 'like honey in a flower', but when the supreme incarnates, the incarnation is 'all honey'.

Aurobindo (1872-1950): 'Because the spiritual progress of humanity requires external support, God manifests himself so that we feel divinity is something close to humanity and available as an example.'

Historical Crux

Though Hindus believe that the Supreme being (usually thought of as Vishnu in this context) has ten incarnations, nine accomplished and one yet to come, clearly not all can be thought of as complete incarnations. Few Hindus would accept the stories of God incarnating as a fish, a tortoise, a boar, a man-lion, or a dwarf as full incarnations. They come, at best, within the categories 2-4 on Ramanuja's list above. The four human incarnations, Parasurama, Rama, Krishna and Buddha, all look more promising, though generally only Krishna (and perhaps Rama) are usually regarded as 'God in the flesh'. Buddha was the founder of a great religion, but he was not God and never claimed to be.

How does this equate with Christian belief that God has come in full human form only once, in the person of Jesus Christ?

The answer perhaps lies in the nature of the stories in which the accounts of Krishna (and Rama's) incarnations occur. The *Ramayana* and the *Mahabharata* are epic poems, uncovering profoundly important eternal truths in mythological form. These truths relate to right ways of living, and are expounded through delightful allegories and metaphors, that are put across with great vibrancy.

They are expounded in epic stories of courage and adventure: Who could forget the heroic exploits of the Pandava brothers in their struggles to regain the kingdom that is rightfully theirs? How could the reader's heart not go out to Rama's bride, a captive of the evil king of Sri Lanka? These mythologies are profoundly important for Asian culture, because of their great moral teaching and the grounding they provide in social ethics. Yet, at the end of the day, they are stories. *They didn't really happen, and Krishna and Rama were never 'real' people.*

Like all great mythologies, they tell timeless truths in the guise of fiction. The historicity of the stories is unimportant; it is the eternal truths they convey that are all important. For Sankara, for example, it is not the lower level of *maya* or earthly events that is important, but the higher level of eternal truth, righteousness and *dharma*.

Amongst the philosophical undercurrents explored within these epic tales - and indeed elsewhere, in the Upanishads and other religious texts - is the idea of the nature of God. What is he like? In this exploration, the learned sages debate and examine the concept of 'What would God be like if he came to earth as a man?' Many conclusions are reached, often contradictory.

The stories of Krishna's amourous exploits with the gopis, and his mistress Radha, were stories intended to explore the consequences of being God on earth. These sexually promiscuous liaisons that are an embarrassment to many pious Hindus, seek only to show that beyond any possibility of being tainted by *karma* or sin, God on earth could do what he jolly well wanted! The Bible takes a different stance, teaching that God on earth would not seek to abuse such immunity to his own moral laws.

The incarnation of Jesus Christ, is the actual fulfillment of a 'myth' - it is a historical event that really happened; *it was through Jesus Christ alone that God really lived on earth as a man.* For Christ's followers, the eternal truths have vital importance to everyday living. The moral teaching and social ethics are crucial; but historians have convincing evidence that Jesus was a real person, and not simply an archetypal hero of fiction - the Superman or Batman of his day.

The trustworthiness of the historical record is confirmed by specific, documented, archaeological discoveries. The written records too can be empirically tested; it can be shown that if the Bible is dismissed as historically unreliable then, on the same criteria, all classical literature and historical records must be dismissed and history disregarded. Many of the accounts of Christ were written by his critics, unintentionally confirming that he was indeed a figure of history!

Historian F.F. Bruce in *The Books and the Parchments* writes: 'It cannot be too strongly asserted that in substance the text of the Bible is certain... the number of manuscripts of the New Testament, of early translations from it, and or quotations from it in the oldest writers of the Church, is so large that it is practically certain that the true reading of every doubtful passage is preserved in some one or other of these ancient authorities. *This can be said of no other ancient book in the world.*'

The oldest copy of any part of the New Testament - the accounts of Jesus and the early Church, written by first-hand sources and eyewitnesses - is the John Ryland MMS, which dates back to

130AD, about a century after Christ's death. The oldest copy of the Old Testamant, the Jewish *Torah* is amongst the famous Dead Sea Scrolls which are more than 2,000 years old. *By comparison, the oldest surviving copies of any Hindu texts are no older then the fifteenth century AD...*

For millenia, India has sailed serenely through the years, almost impervious to outside influence. It's people were unconcerned about 'trivialities' such as historical truth. But now the twentieth century has caught up with South Asia. Not simply for the eighteen million Asians who now live outside the sub-continent, but for the homeland itself - now firmly part of the modern era - history has finally arrived.

In an age of technology, education and international commerce, it is no longer adequate to be unconcerned about sources of knowledge. A businessman would not dream of buying a consignment of mythical jodhpurs that didn't really exist. A scientist cannot examine Arjuna's chariot because it exists only as part of a philosophical thesis about *bhakti*.

The mythical can be intensely personal, but only a God who is *real* in every sense of the word can have the power to help the suffering individual. Christians believe that there are strong arguments to support the claim that only in Christ did Isvara become the only 'God in the flesh' to have truly come in the flesh!

*'I can truthfully say that I am slow
to see the blemishes of fellow human beings,
being full of them myself.'
- Gandhi*

KARMA:*Why am I so distant from divinity?*

Hindus are often very upright and proud people, reluctant to take charity from anyone. Asians hate being in debt and take pride in paying their bills promptly and in full. Pious Hindus believe that they will have to pay for all their sins and transgressions - their *karmic debt* - themselves, over thousands of lifetimes.

Thinking and pondering ways to pay debts is a common Asian preoccupation. There is an expression used when one Asian sees another Asian sitting in deep thought: 'What *hundi* do you have to pay that you look so worried?' A hundi is a bill! The Hindu view is that 'I have to pay for everything.' That is the bottom line; yet there is no way that he or she will manage to pay the *hundi* of their accumulated sin or *karma*.

'For myself as a Hindu trader, this worry about how the weight of my sins could be paid used to keep me awake night after night,' explains one Asian businessman who later became a follower of Christ. 'It was a tremendous relief to hear the good news of Christ's payment, once and for all, for all my sins. If the Hindu owned the whole universe, it wouldn't be enough to pay the *hundi*; the creator of the universe had to give his very self. The only one who could pay it - the supreme God himself - has paid the debt, and written **Paid in Full** across the bottom of the bill. A man *must*, but only God *can* pay the wages of sin.'

That's a very confident statement! Before we consider the Christian position in detail, let's look at how Hindus believe they too can solve the problem of *karma*:

Guardians of Cosmic Order

Karma, once simply the name for a religious rite, has long since come to mean the idea that one's actions in this life affect one's future destiny for better or worse. It should never be confused with *kama* - a concept relating to sexual gratification!

The doctrine of *karma* is sometimes viewed loosely as 'people being responsible for their actions'. What we sow, we must reap. Yet *karma* is different from mere causality. Causality dictates that every action has consequences simply because the action has been performed; but *karma*'s effects derive from the attitude of the doer. As Krishna teaches Arjuna in the Gita, actions which are performed from duty, in a disintertested way stemming from no desire have no 'karmic effects'.

Good and evil are contrasted in the *Brhadaranyaka Upanishad*: 'According as one acts, according as one behaves, so does one become. The doer of good becomes good. The doer of evil becomes evil. One becomes virtuous by virtuous action, bad by bad action.' *(4.4.5)*

Many modern Asians are openly sceptical about the whole idea of *karma*. Arun Shourie, in *Hinduism: Essence and Consequence*, writes: 'You can comb the Upanishads, the Brahma-Sutra, the Gita for the meaning of karma... and you will not get beyond the following circularity: What is *karma*, you ask, and the answer is: "It is that which explains your present state". "But *what* explains my present state?" you persist; only to be told, "It is your *karma*."' Such circular arguments are not verifiable.

Modern Indian philosopher Radhakrishnan traced the karma concept back to the earlier concept of *rta*, the order seen in nature, but related to the pattern of human conduct. 'The gods were charged with guarding and maintaining this sacred harmony which, as the moral order, provides for humans and gods alike the standards of right conduct,' Burnett explains. 'Although this concept changed to mean simply the correct performance of sacrificial ritual, it supplied the foundation for the development of the law of *karma*.'

For most Asians, of course, *karma* is forever linked with *samsara* - the intimidating belief that the soul after death goes on to live another life in another body, repeating the cycle over and over. *Samsara* will be explored in depth in a chapter of its own. For the moment though, an important problem needs to be addressed concerning *samsara*'s connection with *karma*:

If life has to be lived over and over as a result of *karma* or sins committed in previous lives, when did we first fall prey to *karma*? Surely there must have been a point at the beginning when each soul began its first life with no debt carried over, because it had never lived any earlier lives. Unfortunately, scholars are not too good at answering this tricky question! The idea that the human race was once in a sinless state is seen in Hindu philosophy as 'an abstraction'...

Arun Shourie again: 'We are told that my present state is accounted for not just by the karma-balance I have accumulated in this lifespan, but by the balance I have piled up in my past incarnations too; the latter surely is an unknowable Swiss account if ever there was one!

'It should now be clear that the sequence in which these concepts evolved was not that these laws or phenomena or entities - *karma*, *maya*, *rta* and the like - were actually observed in action and then the observer recorded their existence and operation for us. What happened was that some empirical phenomena - whether it was the orderliness of the stars or the privations of the good and hardworking - could not be explained away, and so black boxes were invented to "explain" them. These boxes, as is their want, then acquired lives of their own and came - Frankenstein like - to actually dominate the collective psyche of the community,' espouses Shourie eloquently. For many Hindus, tautologies have to suffice for explanations.

'Close on the heels of tautologous concepts come empty boxes, boxes in which the teacher or the aspirant is himself free to stuff such meanings to suit the occasion. The Upanishads, and they merely examplify the tradition in this respect, manufacture a number of these boxes. The words, rituals, concepts that are so invented are extremely useful - they are the best aids for self-hypnosis, for the devotee himself endows them with "meaning" and then comes to believe that the "meaning" is inherent in them, that this is indeed *their* meaning.'

The trouble with a view of *karma* which depends on debt supposedly accrued in 'previous lives' is that 'the rich can now rest assured that the poor have only themselves to blame for their present state or that nothing but the latter's past misdeeds have landed them where they are. They can now congratulate themselves as having been certified as "meritorious-on-balance" by the Lord, the ledger-keeper himself.'

Clearly we have to be very careful of non-verifiable double-think if we are to get to the bottom of *karma*. In attempting to use *karma* to justify the inequality of the caste system, many have performed verbal somersaults and semantic cartwheels. We need to explain *karma* without recourse to unproven concepts which - like *samsara* -have little credence within the Vedic tradition, or much intellectual credibility for an educated person brought up away from the superstitious hotbed of the Indian sub-continent.

Instant Karma!

If an Asian vegetarian, perhaps at a party or a reception, learns that the food he has consumed has meat within it, a typical reaction will not be 'Oh, I feel terrible'. The deed is already done, so they will probably say, 'Oh, one more sin to pay for.' One more debit to the cosmic balance sheet. A good deed will have to be done to make recompense, to balance a bad deed with a good one, for such is the unescapable law of *karma*.

Eating meat is thought to be particularly bad for your *karma*, because animals have karma, and by eating their bodies you are taking on their karma too, and making the situation even worse for yourself. The concept is actually borrowed from Jainism and is not authentic to Hindu belief in its original form; during the Vedic period, even the priests tucked into a plate of meat with great vigour!

Many Hindus believe now that it is best to avoid any hurt to any living creature. This *ahimsa* or non-violence principle - also derived from Jainism - is often taken to ridiculous extremes. Combined with the principle of destiny, or *lekhio* - the idea that 'everything is written' - it produces an appallingly fatalistic view of life.

Typical Hindus, Ravi and his family are devout followers of Krishna. In one corner of their tiny flat in downtown Manila, pictures of the doe-eyed, blue-skinned god stand around a small family altar. For him, religion means a set of rules to help him to live life in a modest way, without offending anyone. 'We have to speak the truth at all times,' he says as an example of how the family's faith affects daily living. 'I don't eat meat,' is one of the legalistic rules that Sankara would love. The whole family are looking forward to Diwali this year, when the priest will come and bless the financial accounts of the small family business, signing them with the holy *mantra* 'Om'. Being a follower of Krishna is little different from cherishing any of the other major deities. Ravi is a typical Hindu, who will probably think about going on a pilgrimage at some point in his life.

A pilgrimage may be made to some holy place or shrine, with a view to acquiring some positive *karma* to offset the negative. In *Approaches to Hinduism*, Jackson and Killingley explain: 'Some pilgrims come to ask for a cure, for the birth of a son, or some other boon. Some come in fulfillment of a vow; a mother, for instance, may have promised the deity of the place that if her sick child recovered she would perform an austere pilgrimage and make an offering. Another purpose is purification from sins, removing the guilt of past deeds, either from the pilgrim himself or from his ancestors. The pilgrim may seek freedom from past deeds in general, or believe that some misfortune is a result of an unknown sin committed in a previous life, and can be remedied by washing away the sin. Or the pilgrimage may take a particularly arduous form, such as following a prescribed route round the sacred place, touching the ground with one's body all the way.'

Christianity, too, has a strong tradition of pilgrimages, though with scant biblical backing. In the modern day, this seldom amounts to more than religious tourism, visiting the holy sites in Israel. In medieval times, arduous overland pilgrimages were taken at great risk, in the (false) belief that they would attract spiritual merit. Self-abuse (through excessive fasting or flagellation of the body) was once similarly rampant, but has long since almost totally died out - as it doing in Hindu practice, particularly in the west.

The belief that repentance is possible, but that it must be accompanied by payment - cash on the nail if the sin is to be absolved - is common to Hinduism and Christianity over millenia of their history. The above are all ways in which people have tried in vain to pay the price of sin.

It's a Sin

When examined without the intimidating presupposition of reincarnation, *karma* is actually close to the concept of sin as found in the semitic faiths of Judaism, Christianity and Islam. Indeed, the word 'sin' appears, meaning *karma*, in the works of many Hindu writers.

Vaishnava Brahmin, in his *gayatri mantra*, humbly offers the prayer: 'I am a sinner, a doer of sin, a sinful self, born in sin.

O God, save me and take away all my sins.' A Muslim poet has written: 'What is life, but the sin of Adam; If I have life, I am a sinner.'

Radhakrishnan once remarked: 'We have sin with us from the beginning of our history, but we have recently begun to worship it.' Such foolish behaviour when the Holy Bible warns that 'The wages of sin are death,' and the *Mandala Brahmopanishad* confirms that, 'the fruit of sin is Hell.'

A disciple of Ramakrishna (1834-86) said of his guru: 'We admired him and loved him, and it is no exaggeration to say that we were loved in return. The sense of sin was very acute in him. Often we heard him earnestly supplicating God for forgiveness and mercy.'

In Sanskrit, many words are used to signify 'sin': *agas, enas* (offence) *adhidroha, drugdha* (malicious, treacherous) *kilbisa, repas* (stain) *rina* (debt) and the general word for sin, *papa*, though this comes without ethical connotations. Moral evil is denoted by the words *agha* and *amhas*, and in the Vedic hymns as *anrta*. There are many more. We will do better to examine *karma* seeing it as synonymous with 'sin', rather than an adjunct to an unproven philosophical theory like reincarnation.

Sin is closely connected with the notion of evil. The Christian 'holy man' St Augustine distinguished between the evil that one *does* in disobeying God, which is the sin itself; and the evil that one *suffers*, which is punishment for those sins. Theologian John Hick considers that evil can have three forms: physical pain, mental suffering and moral wickedness.

Both Hindus and Christians agree that the problem of evil does not come from God but from humanity. Because the cause of evil is seen differently, so the solutions differ - though not to so great an extent as one might imagine.

One problem with the Hindu response - *samsara* - is that it leaves God out of the picture, unless he is seen simply as a supervisor of the operation of *karma*: the director of all sentient beings in a series of actions resulting in consequences that are consistent with their past conduct and character. There is little scope for free will.

Prakash says: 'The sheer necessity of the *karma* doctrine appears to have arisen over the understanding that nothing can explain the cause of evil and suffering in the world, except they are related to the previous deeds of the *jiva* (soul)... In this doctrine, there is no means of knowing why you or I may be suffering any particular rebirth, neither is there any opportunity for us to correct past deeds or mistakes in the future.'

The *Nyaya* school of Hindu philosophy weds the inexorable law of *karma* with compassion. God can be sublimely merciful without compromising the moral laws of *karma*, because 'moral law is the law of God's own being', so mercy cannot subvert it. It is a sign of his grace, a response in which - perhaps surprisingly - Hinduism and Christianity are in full agreement. Both traditions agree that repentance is required before grace can become effective.

Guilt and Repentance

In the *Rig Veda* can be found prayers and petitions that the guilt-ridden might be freed from guilt. While the fire god Agni is specifically the guardian of ritual order, Varuna - at that point in the development of Hinduism - was seen as the god of moral order, and it is to him that many of the prayers or incantations were directed. Varuna was a law-giver as stern in instructing Manu, the Hindu law-bringer, as Yahweh was with Moses and the people of Israel. Varuna was angered by sin and the infringement of his ordinances, which he promised to punish severely. Some Christian commentators have seen a reflection of their own deity in Varuna, whose prime responsibility it was to uphold moral law, and to whom people earnestly prayed for deliverance from sin and culpable guilt.

The Vedic hymn writers pleaded for forgiveness, but by the period of the *Brahmanas* (approx 1000 BC) it was considered that forgiveness was not possible without repentance *and* sacrifice - though sacrifice was no longer performed as a gift to the gods, either to appease them or to win their favour. 'Sacrifice became, so to say, a cure for sin,' explains Dhavamony. It was a mystic sacrament of redemption.

The whole set up became so elaborate that expiatory rites (*prayacitta*) were performed to remedy errors made during the other sacrifices. The rites corresponded to two concepts of sin: transgression of the will of heavenly beings, or sin as a substance which adheres to the sinner and which must be washed away.

Often, expiation required merely the repetition of a formula such as that in the *Satapatha Brahmana*: 'Whatever sin we have committed in the village or in the forest, in company or by ourselves, that we expiate by sacrifice.'

There are, then, also sins that lie outside ritual performance, and which are committed in everyday life. the *Tai Hiriya Brahmana* and the *Vajasneya Samhita* contain forms of repentance: 'What with our voice we have spoken improperly... what we have committed improperly with our voice, with our mind, with our arms, with our thighs, with our knees..."...deliver me from that sin and all distress.' These prayers - which are not dissimilar to prayers said by many Christians - would have been offered up to personal deities in worship through hundreds of years of Asian history.

Puja, the worship of deity, of course remains the rite most performed in the present day. Commonly, after a minor deity has been placated, a prayer is said to the Supreme God, addressing him as great God, Lord, truthful one, real existence, one without a second, the protector, the unshaken and the immovable. Significantly, when worshipping the supreme deity, unlike the lesser 'gods', Hindu practice does not require that God be evoked, welcomed or bade farewell - he is, after all, eternally everywhere.

Devotion, or *sraddha*, is needed to make offerings and prayers for forgiveness effective. The *Bhagavad Gita* affirms, 'Faith is superior to the merit born of (*Vedic*) recitations and meditations. An act violated by defect of speech is saved by faith. But neither speech nor mind can save an act that is violated by want of faith.'

In the Christian tradition too, faith is the hallmark of the true believer. The superiority of faith over works is spoken of many times by that Christian 'guru' St Paul in his writings. 'When a man works, his wages are not credited to him as a gift, but as an obligation. However, to the man who does not work but trusts God who justifies the wicked, his faith is credited as righteousness.' *(Romans 4:4,5)*

Paul speaks frequently of being 'justified' or 'made right with God' by grace, through faith alone: 'A righteousness from God apart from law has been made known, to which the Law and the Prophets testify. This righteousness from God comes through faith in Jesus Christ to all who believe. There is no difference, for *all have sinned and fall short of the glory of God*, and are justified freely by his grace through the redemption that came by Christ Jesus.' *(Romans 3:21-24)*

Amazing Grace

God accepts neither good nor bad *karma*; good works cannot atone for bad, according to Christ's followers - though the Islamic view enables good deeds to be traded off in payment of bad deeds. The *Adi Granth Saheb*, too, depreciates the efficacy of works: 'Release is not possible by effort.'

Because God is the all-knowing *nirguna brahman*, no offence, sin or transgression can be hidden from him. Nothing can 'hide' wrongdoing from his knowledge, nor can he ever forget wrong behaviour. And, as both the Holy Bible and the *Mandala Brahmopanishad* have confirmed above, every misguided and sinful action is punishable by death and hell!

There is a steep price that has to be paid to atone for sin before grace can become effective, by both Hindu and Christian reckoning, but perhaps someone else could pay the price. If an Asian gets into debt and his creditors are clammering for repayment, it is regarded as the responsibility, or *dharma*, of his relatives to help him out. If the man were taken to court by his creditors, it would reflect badly on the whole family, whose social standing, dignity and *izzat* would be at risk. Of course the family will do whatever they can to help!

Works won't work. But, as we saw in the last chapter, *grace* - or unmerited favour bestowed by someone else - is a different matter. 'If you give up your seat on a bus to allow someone who is struggling to stand have your seat, then you take their suffering onto yourself. The cost of your sacrifice is equal to the kindness done.' The same is the case when God bears the penalty of our sin and guilt upon himself, Prakash explains.

One of the clearest illustrations of how God combines justice and mercy is given by Mike Fearon in the book *Martin Luther: The Man Who Lived in Fear*.

'An important judge is presiding at the trial of a man who has committed a serious crime. As the trial progresses, it becomes more and more obvious that the accused is guilty. Then it becomes known that the accused is a childhood friend of the judge. Everyone expects the accused to get let off with a light sentence, because of the long friendship, but when the judge finally pronounces judgement, the whole court is stunned to hear the most severe sentence possible! The convicted man will have to pay a very large fine, or spend many years in prison. There seems to be no way in which he can raise enough money, so prison seems to be the only option.

'Then the judge rises before the court. He takes off his powdered wig, his ermine robes, and all the trappings of his office. He leaves his place of honour at the head of the court and walks down to the lowest station. There, he walks up to the clerk of the court and pays, with his own money, the enormous fine which he himself has imposed only a few moments earlier!

'If he had let off the guilty person, he would have been a corrupt and unworthy judge. But by paying the fine himself, the letter of the law had been upheld and his love for his childhood friend had been expressed in the most costly and loving manner imaginable.'

Divine grace surely dictates that justice has to be done; sin or *karma* cannot simply be forgotten or ignored. In Hinduism - in least in Ramanuja's version of it - grace is thought to be cheap because no one has to pay for it. In Christianity, grace is the most expensive commodity in the universe, because it required Isvara (aka *Saguna Brahman*, or Purusa, God the *avatar*) to die a violent and cruel death, brutally nailed to a wooden cross as a sacrificial victim in place of those destined to receive his grace. The price of grace was literally 'paid on the nail'!

The sixteenth verse of the *purusasukta* shows that the incarnation of God meets its purpose through sacrifice: 'The gods sacrificed Purusa as the sacrifice. This is the earliest established principle. Through this the sages obtained heaven.' The *Rig Veda* expounds this in wonderful poetry: 'When the gods performed a sacrifice with Purusa as an oblation, spring was its melted butter, summer its fuel, and autumn its oblation. They sprinkled Purusa, born in the beginning, as a sacrifice in the straw. The gods, the sadhyas and the seers sacrificed Him as the victim.' *(10:90.6,7)* The fundamental concept of the supreme creator God sacrificed as a just atonement for human sin, is as authentic to Christianity as it is to Hinduism:

The Bible says: 'God predestined Jesus as a sacrifice of atonement, through faith in his blood. He did this to demonstrate his justice, because in his forebearance he had left the sins committed beforehand unpunished - he did it to demonstrate his justice at the present time, so as to be just and the one who justifies the man who has faith in Jesus.' *(Romans 3:25,26)*

Here, the cost of grace was the painful death of the Lord Jesus Christ, Isvara himself paying a price equal to the kindness done. To atone for sin - not simply to hide it, but to remove its effects for ever - *Saguna Brahman* paid the cost levied by *nirguna brahman*.

Just as the judge became an 'ordinary person' to meet the payment required by his own sentence, so God became human in Christ to meet the demands of his own justice:

Christ Jesus, *Saguna Brahman*, 'being in very nature God, did not consider equality with God something to be grasped, but made himself nothing, taking the very nature of a servant, being made in human likeness. And being found in appearance as a man, he humbled himself and became obedient to death - even death on a cross! Therefore God exalted him to the highest place and gave him a name that is above every name, that at the name of Jesus every knee should bow, in heaven and on earth and under the earth, and every tongue confess that Jesus Christ is Lord, to the glory of God the Father.' (*Philippians 2:6-11*)

Of the Purusa, the *Chandogya Upanishad* says, 'This Man is above all sin and one who worships Him and follows Him also raises himself above sin.' (1.6:6,7) In his book *Christ in Ancient Vedas*, Joseph Padinjarekara writes: 'The will of God was to make a perfect sacrifice through the offering of God Himself. For that purpose He needed a body in order to offer this sacrifice on earth. In the *Brhadaranyaka Upanishad* we read that Prajapati, the Supreme God, wished for a body to be offered. This is fulfilled in the incarnation of Jesus. God became flesh and dwelt among us. The Son of God became the Son of Man; Prajapati became Purusa (Man).' And He was delighted to fulfill the will of the Father Almighty, *nirguna brahman*. Ramanuja, of course, made no distiction between *nirguna brahman* and *Saguna Brahman*, and found himself open to criticism.

Madhva and Grace

In not distinguishing between *Saguna Brahman* and *nirguna brahman* - Ramanuja's opponents claim - the ultimate being, majestic and eternal, dwelling in unfathomable brightness, was *directly* connected at the moment of sacrifice with the imperfect bodies and minds of people. So all their imperfections should cling to Brahman, contaminating his untainted purity. This is the major argument that critics have levelled against monism, even in the modified form in which Ramanuja presented it.

The Hindu philosopher Madhva (1238-1317) got around this awkward problem, like many others, by proposing a strict dualist stance. But - unless one resorts to the God-Man concept - this always raises the problem of finding something to link the two realities:

Madhva developed a dualist philosophy, seeing God and the world each as eternal and absolutely real - though both matter and souls (he differentiates between the two) are seen as ultimately dependent upon God for their sustained existence. For him, the Lord 'appears among men to show the path of righteousness.' When a soul faithfully follows the path - and thereby truly perceives and realises the Lord's birth and work - he or she obtains release from the world, or *moksha*.

For Madhva, knowledge of God and his grace were the chief means of salvation. Madhva's views move even further from monism than Ramanuja's standpoint, and theologically they are virtually identical to those of Christianity. For him, the *atman* was a 'mirror image' of God, identical but not the same. In Christian terms, the *atman* and Isvara are equals within the same Godhead. The *atman* is God's Spirit.

God's intimate love for the human who turns to him is spoken of in the Bible and Upanishads alike: 'As a man in the embrace of his beloved wife knows nothing within or without, so the person in the embrace of the conscious *atman* knows nothing within or without.' (*Brihadaranyaka Upanishad*) 'I have come into my garden, my sister, my bride; I have gathered my myrrh with my spice. I have eaten my honeycomb and my honey; I have drunk my wine and my milk. Eat, O friends, and drink; drink your fill, O lovers.' (*Song of Songs 5:1*)

Madhva was openly hostile to Sankara, seeing him as a deceiver. His own philosophical school took the name of Sankara's *advaita* (non-dualist) school, and removed the 'a' to produce *dvaita* (dualist).

The *Dvaita Vedanta* school criticises the *Advaita* school for making God too impersonal. Whereas even Ramanuju placed emphasis on devotion *and* works as means of reaching God, Madhva believed that the supreme being can only be reached by grace - though grace is said to be given only to those who live righteous lives.

The attitude of the Dvaita school is often in agreement with Christian theology, but none of the philosophical schools really solves all the problems. What is needed, is a mid ground between monism and dualism, which will protect God's holiness from the contamination which would occur if he and the world shared in the one divine nature, yet allow one way contact enabling creation to be influenced and sustained by him, and avoid the 'seperate but united' paradox.

The God-Man concept does very nicely, philosophically, because it acts as a valve, enabling direct contact with humanity on the part of the God-Man Saguna Brahman, while protecting the sanctity of nirguna brahman. But theologically, only a doctrine of grace - as proposed by Ramanuja, Madhva and Christian theology - is fully satisfying intellectually and emotionally. Christian belief combines the two.

The Death of God

The implications of Christian belief - and many Hindu texts - are that, when the God-Man died his sacrificial death, the ultimate being *was* directly connected with the imperfect bodies and minds of sinful people, so all the imperfections *did* cling to *Saguna Brahman*, contaminating his purity!

In consequence, *nirguna brahman* preserved his sanctity and holiness by separating himself and turning away. The two who were joined in the one Godhead were sundered, and Isvara cried out, like a son to his father...

'From the sixth hour until the ninth hour darkness came over the land. About the ninth hour Jesus cried out in a loud voice, *"Eloi, Eloi, lama sabachthani?"* - which means "My God, my God, why have you forsaken me?"... And when Jesus had cried out again in a loud voice, he gave up his spirit... The earth shook and the rocks split.' (*Matthew's Gospel 27:45,46,50,51*)

The whole of creation was reviled by the abomination. The sinful nature of the created order had adhered to the one through whom it had been created! God's holy Word, or Vac, *had been defiled by carrying in his essential being the sinfulness of the whole world, and the Supreme Brahman had forsaken the one with whom he intimately shared the divine essence.*

But the grave could not hold God captive. When the cost to atone for sin had been paid by the death of the living God, grace could abound once more. The father *nirguna brahman* raised Jesus from the grave, and he appeared to his *sanyassins* or disciples. 'Then he opened their minds so that they could understand the Scriptures. He told them, "This is what is written: The Christ will suffer and rise from the dead on the third day, and repentance and forgiveness of sins will be preached in his name to all nations..."'

(*Luke's Gospel 24:45-47*)

Hindu texts also affirm that the sacrificial victim would be raised from death, his body reconstructed. A famous verse in the *Kathopanisad* likens supreme God to an inverted tree: 'With roots *above* and the branches *below*, this (manifested Brahma) is as an ancient asvattha tree, that indeed is the bright one that is Brahma, that indeed is called immortal. In Him all worlds are contained, Him verily nothing goes beyond. This is that.' *(6.1)* Taking this image, the Brhadaranyaka Upanishad says, 'If the tree is cut off, it will live again by its root [that is, from above.] The man lives again!' *(3.9.28,4,5)* 'Prajapati put Himself together again by means of the chandas, the Word - the Scriptures,' says the *Aitareya Aranyaka. (3,2.6.2)*

'He is the beginning and the firstborn from among the dead, so that in everything he might have supremacy. For God was pleased to have all his fullness dwell in him, and through him to reconcile to himself all things, whether things on earth or things in heaven, by making peace through the blood, shed on the cross.' (*Colossians 1:18-20*)

St Peter's clear teaching was that people could now come to God in faith and be united with him, through God's grace. 'God has raised this Jesus to life, and we are witnesses of the fact. Exalted to the right hand of God, he has received from the Father the promised Holy Spirit and had poured out what you now see and hear.' (*Acts 2:32,33*)

'One who knows the Purusa becomes free and gains immortality.' *Kathopanisad (1,3.8)*

Karma Chameleon

Some western Asians don't need much persuasion. They reject the doctrines of *karma* and *samsara* just as they reject other social, cultural and religious traditions. Like a chameleon, its ever-changing colours lending it camouflage and enabling it to blend into the background, many Asians are now changing their religious views in order to blend into western society.

In the west, many nominal Christians have become so indifferent to, and hardened against, the teachings of Christ that the Church no longer plays any meaningful part in their lives. They may attend services for marriages and funerals, and the occasional Christmas or Easter service; but otherwise, they live their lives as though God only existed for a few hours a year, and was imprisoned within the Church building, unable to escape into real life.

For the western Asian, the point is rapidly approaching where the same religious indifference will be true. They will attend temples once or twice a year to placate family members, or because an event of particularly close family significance is taking place there, a wedding perhaps. But to all practical purposes, they will have become secularised.

Many follow *gurus* because it is easier and less time consuming. Some drop away from Hinduism altogether, perhaps to become Buddhists, the acceptable alternative to Hindu faith for many Asian families.

In India, huge numbers are turning to Buddhism as a way of escaping from the rigorous caste system which still permeates Indian life. Gautama the Buddha in an Asian home is simply one more of the idols. In turning to Buddha, they step outside of the caste system which restricts the jobs for which they would be considered eligible. Economic necessity fuels the spiritual compromise.

Many Asians became Roman Catholics in nineteenth century India, because they found it easier to adapt to a form of worship where statues and icons are used - it was culturally familiar. The statue of the madonna and child replaced the idols of Siva in their affections. Rosaries and incense were similarly attractive. Fasting, abstaining from alcohol and paying penance are alike in Catholicism and Hinduism, and there are many other close connections and similarities. Catholicism is still an easier and more accessible option for many Hindus who want to follow Christ, than embracing the teachings of the Bible.

For others, God has died and remains in the grave - if, indeed, he ever really lived for them. The old stories no longer have any cultural relevance for them - if they ever did. They are so totally secularised that they have long since ceased to worry about the concept of their karmic debt. But the heartache and loss of meaning which comes from the loss of the sacred and divine can be an unbearable burden.

Let's look at ways of resurrecting God from the tomb of apathy and indifference, and allow him to step out into the light of daily living...

PART TWO: THE ARROW FLIES

'If moreover God should chastise men
according to their deserts, He would not
leaveeven a reptile on the back of the earth.
But to an appointed time doth he respite them.'
- The Koran (Chapter 35)

CHAPTER

6

KARMA YOGA:
How can ceremonies and ritual help me?

To most people, a 'myth' is simply a story that is not true! Here, we are using the word in the correct way, to describe 'a story that speaks of an ultimate reality in order to answer key questions about the meaning of everyday reality.'

A myth which seems to be about God (or gods) is actually about an 'ultimate reality', in which our concepts of who (or what!) God *is* may really be just an identifying tag. The way we think about God is simply 'the way we think about God'; it is not the *reality* of God. As Radhakrishnan said, 'Every word, every concept is a pointer which points beyond itself. The sign should not be mistaken for the thing signified. The signpost is not the destination.'

The *Ramayana* and the *Mahabharata* are probably the world's longest myths about God, and 'myth' should not be seen here as a derogatory term. Myths are a useful source of metaphor, but they are usually treated very matter-of-factly because the simple stories can reach the heart of a matter in a way that complex philosophical discussions can never achieve. Myths have an important unifying function in Asian life and thought. The rich and poor alike of India frequently talk about characters in mythology as though they were their next door neighbours!

Until about two hundred years ago, the stories of the Bible - particularly those surrounding the festivals of Christmas and Easter - functioned in western Europe in much the same fashion. It's as though our stories of the past give us a foundation without which we cannot survive; they keep us 'human'. Yet today, all our stories are at risk because we no longer live in the comfortable isolation of our ancestors, assuming that our own stories are the only ones that exist.

Many Asians - particularly the urban-educated middle class - no longer feel 'at home' with their mythology. Many of the myths are openly criticised in modern India on historical or moral grounds in a way that would never have happened even fifty years ago. Fabulous stories of talking animals, monkey gods, magic potions and the like seem to lack a sophistication that sticks in the craw of the educated person. Their own culture clashes with, rather than being validated by, the culture of the legends.

'They and their myths no longer speak the same language,' says Roger Hooker. 'This can create anxieties, for when the myths are lost, or are no longer reliable in the old way, it seems as though the world has come to an end, and in a way it has.' We need new dreams today...

'Most Hindus interpret their lives against a backdrop of myth. These stories that everyone knows create identity; they authenticate social occasions and rituals; they afford precedents and models for ethnic decisions; they provide a common universe of discourse which does much to bind society together. They are a rich quarry for metaphor and allusion. More profoundly, they always seem to point beyond themselves to what, rather loosely, we call a "transcendental dimension of life".

In attempting to preserve the tales by reducing them to factual statements as though they were historical documents - and then perhaps finding them unprovable - their whole meaning is destroyed. But if they were never factual stories in the first place, but allegories and parables, they should never lose their meaning in transmission through the years.

Myths reflect social order. Erosion of fables and allegories mean that language is reduced to the level of secular materialism, and the story of Rama and Sita suddenly has no more meaning than a recipe on the back of a packet of breakfast cereal. Without myths, we can suddenly find ourselves unsure of our place in the social order.

Mythical stories are needed to bond the disparate feelings and concerns of society; now more than ever. In reviewing our earlier book **Sari 'n' Chips**, *The Asian Weekly* commented: 'The British Asian doesn't have it easy. Like Trishanku caught in limbo between two worlds, he is neither here nor there. In an alien world, Asians who are so deeply tradition bound, find living in Britain a bewildering experience.' It's ironical that, the more the years roll by, the harder it will become for second and third generation Asians to identify with the mythological allegory used above to illustrate their plight!

Under Pressure

Western Asians, and those who dwell in India's big cities, often feel tension between the demands of society that they should marry, have sons, and fulfil an allotted place in the social order; yet renounce that self-same social order and fulfil a spiritual destiny. In the first view, society is a network of obligations, while in the second it is an obstacle in the path of spiritual progress.

No wonder many Asians turn their backs on religion altogether - in a world that has lost the significance of its mythology, and where dreams have lost their magic, secularism often seems the only way to resolve the paradox. The man says, 'I'll just make money and leave religion to my wife'; while the woman says, 'I'll do my spiritual duty and leave the rest to my husband.' Typically, the male's role is to commission the ceremonies from priests, to encourage their family to attend, and not to deter religious practices. It's regarded as a privilege to have a priest in the house, performing rites for the deceased and the living.

Thought of God may well be put off for many years. Perhaps the obligatory paying of a Hindu priest to perform some rituals for the family now and again, will keep God at bay till there is more time to fathom out what is to be done about him! Hinduism is said to have four possible goals: *dharma*, or ethical behaviour; *artha*, or the attainment of worldly goods; *kama*, the fulfilment of sexual urges and procreative activity; and *moksa*, the liberation from attachment or desire. One at a time is usually enough!

These goals can be met in each of the four traditional stages of life: *brahmacharya*, the pursuit of knowledge and wisdom; *gryhasta*, the age of marriage, home building and performing duties to society; *vanaprastha*, or retirement from worldly affairs, handing over to sons so that time can be spent seeking spiritual welfare through study and meditation; and finally *sanyas*:

In this fourth stage, a man is expected to cut himself off completely from the world and wander from place to place on a pilgrimage, preparing for the ultimate detachment of *moksa*. As many of us know, in practice in the west, few Hindus get beyond the first two stages, and the man who manages all four is a rarity indeed. **Karma'n'Chips** will perhaps redress this, and lead many people further along on the traditional quest for God, by making a way clearer.

Even if the prospect of becoming a *sanyassin* seems too daunting - though even westerners are doing it these days - an elderly Hindu approaching his end days, will at least begin to think about trying to work out his salvation. He has married, had children, and looked after his parents in their old age. His daughters are married, and the grandchildren provided for. The point comes where he says 'Now, let's look to my soul!' At that point, the Hindu often begins to look deeper at the origins of his faith, its teaching through the ages, and what it can teach him now in his declining years that may help him in his search for the best way to secure his spiritual destiny.

He may, at that point, encounter the various pathways on which Asians have sought to get near God. The primary ways, *margas* or *yogas*, are *karma yoga*, *jnana yoga*, *bhakti yoga* and *raja yoga*, though there are many more less frequently travelled routes. Even Buddhism, Jainism or Christianity offer attractive prospects to some Hindu seekers of truth in their old age. (Some Asians will have to make an earlier start, as children's exposure to other faiths at school may lead to profound questions which the blighters will expect their all-knowing parents to be able to answer!)

Even in the west, some senior Asian men may make all the preparations they can for their family's future - they will try to do as much good as they can, and avoid as much bad as possible - then they will reach the crucial point of addressing the question of purification of their own souls. A handful take the task seriously enough to leave their families and go to the Himalayas to become *sanyassins*. There, they will try to keep to the spiritual laws, and stay away from contact with anything that might cause them to sin.

But are there not perhaps better ways? To be morbid for a moment, what's going to happen if they 'peg out' too soon? Good intentions will be of little use once your ashes are scattered on the Ganges; or if you are in the grave, pushing up daisies before your time! Better to try a little now, than to plan to do a lot later and not make it.

New dreams cannot be won without effort, and a fresh mythology for western Asians cannot come about overnight. The struggle needs to begin at once, if there is to be time to see it through in this generation of change that is so pregnant with hope. Western

Asians need to say to themselves: 'Will our children forgive us if we leave them with the mess of shattered religious yearnings that are no nearer being pieced into a structure that will really work for Asians in the west than they were when they first arrived on these shores?'

We've seen where we're coming from and what the problems are. Let's get cracking!

A Universal Mythology

To abandon the ways of South Asia entirely will create schism within the Asian community in the west, yet to hold to nothing except that which was developed in the fertile Asian soil will deprive Asian children of a future in the west. A synthesis is needed that keeps as much as possible of the spirituality and culture of the homeland; everything that is - or can be made - compatible with the culture and spirituality of the lands in which Asians find themself. It won't be easy, and it will entail sacrifice, but how is anyone to live without dreams that work?

That's the bad news. The good news is that the fables and mythologies of the east generally have a high degree of compatibility with the more history-based religious stories that give meaning to people of the west - or at least to those westerners who comprehend and seek to live by the teachings of these stories. Since these Bible stories all originated in the middle east - considerably nearer to India than to any western country - that is hardly surprising.

One of the strongest of these 'stories-with-a-meaning' is that of Adam and Eve, found in *Genesis*, the first book of the *Holy Bible*. This tale explains that God put Adam and Eve (the first man and woman) in an earthly paradise, the garden of Eden watered by four rivers - one of which might just possibly be the Indus. They were allowed to eat fruit from any tree they liked, except for the tree of the knowledge of good and evil.

'When the woman saw that the fruit of the tree was good for food and pleasing to the eye, and also desirable for gaining wisdom, she took some and ate it. She also gave some to her husband, who was with her, and he ate it. Then the eyes of both of them were opened, and they realised that they were naked; so they sewed fig leaves together and made coverings for themselves. Then the man and his wife heard the sound of the Lord God as he was walking in the garden in the cool of the day, and they hid from the Lord God among the trees of the garden.' (*Genesis 3:6-8*)

This, in Judaeo-Christian terms, accounts for how *sin* first came into the world - in Hindu terms, it is perhaps how *karma* first began. It explains that we each have 'original sin' with us when we are born, simply through being descendants of the first man. *Saguna Brahman* (or *Yahweh Elohim*, as the original Hebrew has it) cannot be evaded, and the couple are rebuked for breaking the first and only law that had been laid upon them: 'The Lord God made garments of skin for Adam and his wife and clothed them... So the Lord God banished him from the garden of Eden to work the ground from which he had been taken.' (*Genesis 3:21,23*)

To have made the animal skin clothing which symbolically 'covered up' but did not remove the sin, an animal must have been killed. Grace does not come cheaply; in this instance, even to *cover* sin cost a life. (To *atone* for sin cost *Saguna Brahmin* his life...)

Here is the first recorded incidence of the sacrificial system which became refined into tens of thousands of words of laws and commandments found in the Jewish scriptures, the *Torah*, and in millions of words of amplification and commentary in non-scriptural books like the *Talmud*. This sacrificial system is of similar antiquity to the original Hindu sacrificial system, now known as *karma-yoga*.

Both the *Bible* and the *Mahabharata* attribute the origins of sin to a metaphorical tree! 'There is a wonderful tree called desire in the heart of man. It is born of the seed called error. Wrath and pride constitute its large trunk. The wish for action is the basin around its foot (to hold the water to nourish it). Ignorance is the root of that tree, and heedlessness is the water that gives it sustenance. Envy constitutes its leaves... That foolish man who nourishes the tree by indulging in the objects of the senses is destroyed by those very objects in which he indulges.' (*Mahabharata 12.154.1*)

A wise person does not taste the fruit, but destroys the tree. The text goes on to explain that acts undertaken for personal gain or sense gratification lead to enslavement to possessions and sensual pleasure. One 'succeeds in transcending all sorrows' by not eating the fruit of that tree.

The eastern and western accounts then, are not too dissimilar in their allegories. Both are now usually interpreted metaphorically.

An Asian 'Eden'

There is, in Hindu belief, a concept close to that of 'original sin' in Christianity. The *Satapatha Brahmana* says that a person has no right even to live. Simply by being born, one's very being is 'enslaved' by a debt which cannot be repaid. God's breath or spirit animates us; it comes from him and we owe it back to him, but if we return it, we will be dead! The cost of a life can only be another life. In sacrificing an animal, a man, in the words of Hindu scripture, 'redeems himself from death'; his sacrifice itself becomes his spiritual body in the next world. After redeeming himself from death, he must then go on to redeem himself from sin - which he can only do by meeting the demands of the laws of *karma*.

A system of ritual sacrifice came about which sought to emulate the first sacrifice of Purusa, which we examined in chapter three, through which the world came to exist. The problem was that (as H. W. Tull explains in *The Vedic Origins of Karma*) the death and destruction implicit in the original event created a situation where the sacrificer would have to offer up his or her own life to meet the demands. In practice, various effigies or substitutes were employed in place of the sacrificer's own body.

The correctness of the sacrifice later came to symbolise good actions which could atone for bad *karma*. The Upanishads eventually came to interpret this tradition to mean that a life filled with charitable giving and selfless activity is the true meaning of the sacrificial system.

Consequently, most Vedic sacrifices have now lapsed in their literal sense. The *Panch Mahayajna* ritual, involving the offering of food to idols remains popular. But the *Aswamedha Yajna*, or 'horse sacrifice' which can only be performed by a powerful king, and the *Visvajit* which requires the performer to own at least 112 head of cattle, are now well beyond the resources of most people.

As we have seen, in the Vedic period, sacrifice was literally an offering; but by the period of the *Brahmanas*, it had become a means of controlling the gods who were dependent upon sacrifices for their survival! The chief quest in the *Upanishads*, was to understand the sublime nature of God, living in timeless bliss. But it must be understood that this position evolved in response to the earlier Brahmin period of sacrificial mysticism that came close to sorcery.

The sacrifices were believed to possess a mysterious power

capable of modifying the workings of the universe to the advantage of the individual, the basis of modern witchcraft. Even the *Rig Veda* came to be seen as a *grimoire*, or book of spells. The worship of *devas* and nature spirits which ensued was of a type condemned by the biblical prophets as stealing the honour due to the most high God and giving it to his created emissaries.

Easily the most well-known biblical condemnation is the third of the so-called *Ten Commandments*, of which even the most secularised westerner has heard: 'You shall not make for yourself an idol in the form of anything in heaven above or on the earth beneath or in the waters below. You shall not bow down to them or worship them; for I Yahweh your God am a jealous God, punishing the children for the sins of the fathers to the third and fourth generation of those who hate me, but showing love to thousands who love me and keep my commandments.' (*Exodus 20:4*)

'If the sacrifices were performed with the strictest accuracy, then the material advantages for which they were performed were bound to come regardless of the good will or ill will of the gods to whom the prayers were offered,' explains Dasgupta in *Hindu Mysticism*. Mistakes could have fatal consequences. Tvashtar prayed for a son who would *kill* the god Indra. In getting his pronunciation slightly wrong, he ended up with a son who would *be killed* by Indra!

Later, meditation substituted for the virtual 'casting of occult spells', and the mystical power came to be seen as residing in 'specific ways of thinking', rather than in a set of words that had dried up on some page. Symbolism replaced literal meaning everywhere. For example, the literal 'three bruisings of the sacrificial soma plant' came to symbolise three periods of human life. The actual rituals were abandoned in favour of the activities they were believed to have represented. It's as though the leopard had managed to change its spots!

Belief in the effectiveness of the sacrificial system is now almost dead in Hindu belief in the west, but there are still many people in modern India (particularly in the villages) for whom the repetition of arcane mystic formulas is believed to be capable of changing reality. An echo of the old rites remain in many of the commonly practiced domestic ceremonies, such as marriage, and the rituals which follow the death of a family member.

Janaki Abhisheki sounds a note of warning: 'Modern scholarship has tended to fall into the trap of regarding the Veda merely as a source of information for social and other conditions of life existing at that age. It should not be forgotten that the Veda is primarily a spiritual work and meant for man's spiritual uplift.' Misused, the Vedic tradition can also be used for oppression.

Rural 'Hinduism'

In India's 600,000 villages, many practices can still be found which have long since been abandoned in more enlightened places. Some of these practices relate to ritual Hinduism as it was once followed 2,500 years ago when priests were practising sorcerers. Other rites are darker and possibly predate the religious system which became the *sanatana dharma*.

The entire tribal population of South Asia is non-Aryan by race and never came - except in small numbers - under the brahminical *sanatana dharma* tradition, because of geographical isolation. These are the millions who are erroneously called 'Hindu' in the Censuses, but actually follow their ancient tribal faiths:

Shamanism is very common amongst the tribals, practised by witchdoctors who claim to have direct contact with gods and spirits, and able to send their own spirits into another world to summon aid to know the secret things. Drugs, drumming, dancing and chanting are used to achieve a state of altered reality.

Some people in the villages are believed to be born with evil potency in their eyes; simply by gazing at cattle, crops, or other people, they are able to inflict a terrible curse. Belief in *lycanthropy* is rampant - heads of some families claim they can change themselves into animals by sprinkling special water, from magical springs; the belief is very common in tribal society, as is witchcraft - the black art applied for the purpose of harming other people. The superstitious believe in magicians with the ability to go out in spirit, travel great distances instantaneously, and change into animal forms. Often a witch eats internal organs of a dead person or animal, and is believed to be in league with the *devas* or gods.

Magic is traditional, manipulative, and has a definite and concrete goal. It is a private matter unlike religion, and often a paid professional/client relationship exists, where the client believes that rites and spells can achieve specific ends.

Totemism exists throughout the world - certain tribal names in Arabia, for example, indicate the one-time practice of totemism by those tribes, and some scholars think that the ancient Hebrews also dabbled in totemism - but it is particularly strong in South Asia.

There are believed to be upwards of thirty-five tribal groupings in India who practice totemism, including the *Mundeas*, *Horo* and *Hao* tribes.

Fetishism is very popular. A fetish can be any object - perhaps a piece of stone or a stick - anything which can be the potential dwelling place of an evil spirit. The object is closely associated with control of black magic, because the spirit confers its power on the person who possesses it. It can therefore be the basis of a religion involving the worship of objects. There are two types of fetish, natural and artificial. A natural fetish could be a beak, a bone, a claw, or a stick. A strange-shaped stone fetish is most common.

'When such a stone is found, the stone is washed carefully, held between the palms and breathed upon,' writes A W Longchar in *The Tribal Religious Traditions of North East India.*

'If it is an active fetish it will become moistened, but if the fetish is inactive or bad, it will not produce any moisture but will appear dry. This kind of fetish is not kept by anybody, but rather is disposed of carefully so that no unfortunate person will find it. Possessing a bad fetish causes misfortune or even death to the possessor. People consider the fetish to be semi-human, possessing personality and will. A fetish can multiply into many and disappear occasionally, it has a sense of hearing and knowing. It is believed to have a feeling and it knows the meaning of anger and resentment, as well as gratitude and kindness.' A fetish is usually kept in a cloth and occasionally oiled with the blood of sacrifices; this is done mainly at harvest time.

Superstition is rampant even in civilised cities such as Allahabad, in Uttar Pradesh, where the people claim to be orthodox Hindus. Those who have lost a prized possession or a loved one bring rice or dhal to the priests who sit in booths on the Ganges river bank. The priests charge money to take the rice and dhal and sacrifice it to the spirits of the dead. When this has been done, the supplicant often shaves his head in homage.

'Whatever we do, we do it for those who have died, that they might go to heaven,' they say. For the priests, it's a good way of making money - they snatch rupees and extract fees for meaningless rituals, claiming that it will help the departed soul. Relatives are encouraged to 'complete the karma' of those who have died without fulfilling their *karma* themselves; and they go ahead with the ritual for fear that the departed spirits might come back and haunt the living. This is a type of mythology that is far from true Hinduism, and which India would do better without.

Metaphoric Interpretations

King David understood that the temple sacrifices had a metaphorical as well as a mystic significance: 'You do not delight in sacrifice, or I would bring it; you do not take pleasure in burnt offerings. The sacrifices of God are a broken spirit; a broken and contrite heart, O God, you will not despise. In your good pleasure make Zion prosper; build up the walls of Jerusalem. Then there will be righteous sacrifices, whole burnt offerings to delight you; then bulls will be offered on your altar.' (*Psalm 51:16-19*) Clearly both the literal and symbolic meanings are equally valid, in their correct contexts.

In Judaism, none of the temple sacrifices are still perpetuated - largely because Moslims have built a mosque on the only site where sacrifices are allowed according to the *Torah*. Yet Jews are devout about taking the symbolic meaning of the sacrifices, and being generous givers of both their time and money, in service to the community and the synagogue.

It is similar with Hindu sacrifices. A few of the rituals are still in common usage, but most are only practised literally in rural villages. The symbolism has come to be the most important aspect of the sacrificial system, completely overshadowing the mystic significance. 'Sacrifices' are to be performed in everyday life by Hindus - like the Jews - by being generous givers of both time and money to communal and religious service.

'Karma Yoga enjoins upon the aspirant the need to perform actions in the spirit of complete disinterestedness,' says Singh, in *Atman and Moksa*. 'He must ungrudgingly and unconditionally perform all those duties that are particular to his station in society. However, all such duties are to be performed with a view to be worthy of his grace and mercy. All such deeds lead to purification of affections (*atma-shuddhi*). There are also certain specific karmas the performance of which in a spirit of disinterestedness is also included in this discipline, such as the worship of idols as taught in the Agmas, repeating sacred formulae and so on.'

Primarily, karma-yoga today involves making sure that the priests get paid, and in fulfilling one's dharma. Just as sacrifices had to be made in an absolutely correct manner, now the whole of life has to be absolutely correct down to the smallest action. When the religious side intrudes, it is usually in a manner strongly influenced by everyday living. There are now strong worldly strains in Hinduism as practiced in Asian cities, and in the west: prayers are said for new silk saris, jewels and business success! In rural areas, it is a different matter.

Swami Saraswati says, 'It is very easy for Europeans to practice karma-yoga; they are quite close to it, because they like hard work... But what many of them lack is love, the spiritual love which knows no egotism, and gives happiness and bliss... Most Indians, on the other hand, are far from karma-yoga. When Europeans start working, there is no end - and when Indians start talking spirituality, there is no end!'

Practical Karma Yoga

Rural Hinduism - and not just religious practices that we have seen to have nothing to do with the true *sanatana dharma* - is alive and well in the villages of India. For the ordinary man, his chosen god is real. The academics often fail to notice that the people's faith and spirituality doesn't always follow the routes and paths which the text books have decided it should. Visits to the great Hindu temples, many of them as old as fifteen hundred years, still stand high on the list of religious practices in India.

'It has always seemed to me a strange thing that in accounts of Hinduism, even by considerable scholars there is often no mention of Temple worship, and yet the temples have stood in their places for at least thirteen or fourteen hundred years, and they are by no means dead, or empty now,' says Ellis Shaw in *Rural Hinduism*. It is probable that the vast field of Hindu sacred literature has been enough to keep scholars occupied, without the sociological field research that would reveal the ways in which Hinduism is actually practiced 'in the raw' as it were. Professors of Hinduism often know nothing of the gods worshipped by the many millions of their own countrymen, says Ellis.

The young village girl who goes with an offering of milk for the cobra who lives in the anthill under the banyan tree, is as much a contemporary practitioner of the *sanatana dharma* as the Hindu priest who performs the wedding rites in the Grosvenor Hotel, Park Lane, that will unite two powerful international business dynasties.

In Bengal, a *brahmin* priest told Mike Fearon that Hinduism was no longer superstitious. 'It has been reformed,' the priest said, immediately before showing Mike a 'tree of fertility'! 'If a lady has no baby, she will come to this tree to pray for a child,' he explained. 'She will pluck one hair from from her head and use the hair to bind a small stone to the branch of the tree. Then, when she has had a baby, she will come and reclaim the stone. We are trying to free the people from this superstition.'

In 1972, at a temple in Cuttack in Orissa, the presiding goddess Chandi, a form of Durga, was decorated as Kali one night during the great annual festival of Durga Puja (*Navaratri*), which celebrates her victory over the buffalo demon,' C. J. Fuller records in *The Camphor Flame*. He describes how a goat was purified and promised to Chandi by sprinkling it with consecrated water, and worshipped by the Brahmin priests. A ritual prayer was whispered into the sacrificial animal's ear, before its head was severed with a single sword stroke. In one night, some 500 goats had met their end in this way, and their bodies were cooked and eaten by the families on whose behalf the offerings were made. At dawn, the image of Chandi was given a purifying bath, and offered cooked goat meat - though normally only vegetarian dishes are presented to her...

In Calcutta in 1993, a priest at the Kali temple explained: 'People come to give offerings to the gods and the goddess; but it is not necessary to come here, they can worship at home - but it is necessary for them to know how to worship. This is the place of sacrifice. Here we sacrifice black male goats every morning. They are the symbol of the devil,' he explained, though academically Hindus are not supposed to believe in a personal devil!

'We sacrifice them to the goddess Kali. People offering the goat use it as a scapegoat to release them from their problems. After offering the goat, the meat is cooked in our kitchen to feed the poor people.' The ritual has a symbolic spiritual significance, but also a practical value. 'In this temple, we have this system where they know they are not wasting the meat; they know it will go to charity.'

Krishnamurthy, in *Essentials of Hinduism*: 'Just as you have to fill up various forms to get anything done in the civilized world, rituals are the forms which you must fill in order to carry on in the world of spirit. Neither rituals nor penance nor purification rites can themselves deliver the goods. Penance and purification rites are proscribed only for those who have turned away from sin. They come only *after* the change of heart.' No scripture, Hindu or Christian, implies that sin can be removed by means of distribution of gifts or observance of fasts, without an antecedent change of heart, repentence and dependance upon God's grace.

Such changes of heart are reflected in several formal prayers in the *Rig Veda*: 'Forgive the wrongs, committed by our fathers, what we ourselves have sinned in mercy pardon; my own misdeeds do thou O God take from me, and for another's sin let me suffer not.' There are many similar petitions in the Bible.

Fulfillment of Karma-Yoga

Jesus Christ was a good Jew who followed the faith of his ancestors, which involved a sacrificial system every bit as severe and demanding as the old brahminical system. Both systems come up against the same obstacles. Both admit that people deserve to die for their sins, or karmic debt, and look for a perfect high priest to perform a perfect sacrifice that will atone in the sacrificer's place; and both are confounded because the priest doing the sacrificing is himself burdened with bad deeds and unworthy of the task!

Because Christ was the incarnation, the *avatar*, not simply of a lesser god - nor only a partial incarnation of the Supreme Deity, but one in whom the entire fullness of the Godhood was pleased to dwell as *Saguna Brahman* - there was *no way whatsoever in which he could possibly be carrying any karma of his own*. He was Isvara (aka Brahma, Agni and Prajapati) without so much as a hint of sin in him, and thus an ideal sacrifice.

The Bible describes him as a lamb without blemish, who made his one perfect sacrifice once and for all when he sacrificed his own body as an offering potent enough to take away, forever, all the bad *karma* of those who have turned away from sin, trust on the effectiveness of the sacrifice and who put their faith in him.

'Such a high priest meets our needs - who is holy, blameless, pure, set apart from sinners, exalted above the heavens. Unlike the other high priests, he does not need to offer sacrifices day after day, first for his own sins, and then for the sins of the people. He sacrificed for their sins once for all when he offered himself.' (*Hebrews 7:26,27*)

Asian religious texts bear this out. The *Tandya Maha Brahmana* explains that God would offer himself as a sacrifice and obtain atonement for sins. 'God is found in the living body,' says the *Brhd. Ar. Upanishad (4.4.7)*

Perhaps one reason why God bears so many different names in

the Hindu tradition, is that each name signifies a particular role. As Agni, he is lord of the sacrifice - literally the fire that consumes the offering. As Prajapati, he is the sacrificial victim itself. As timeless *nirguna brahman*, he is the one to whom the offering is made. As the deeply personal *Saguna Brahman*, he is the high priest presiding over the ritual.

The *Satapatha Brahmana* explains: 'The gods went on sacrificing unto one another. Prajapati gave himself up to them and the sacrifice became theirs; for indeed the sacrifice is the food of the gods. Having given himself up to the gods, he created that counterpart of himself, to wit, the sacrifice: whence people say, "The sacrifice is Prajapati", for he created it as a counterpart to himself.'

The late Adhyaksha Mandapaka wrote, 'What is evident from all these teachings is that the true and great redeeming sacrifice would be performed by the Sovereign Lord of this world, who putting on both mortality and immortality and becoming incarnate as God-Man, would Himself be the sacrifice to redeem mankind from their sins.' Mandapaka points out that the way in which Christ met his death - bound to a sacrificial post with thorns placed on his head, and nails driven into him - is fully in accord with the *Rig Veda*'s description of the sacrifice.

The similarities between the Vedic pattern and the actuality of Christ's sacrifice as recorded in the Bible are striking. Compare the common features of the following pairs of verses:

- The sacrifice is a public spectacle: 'He who burned out all sins *before all* is Purusa.'*(Brhadaranyaka Upanishad 1.4.1)* Christ was nailed to a cross (crucified) close to a public thoroughfare. 'Poeple passing by shook their heads and hurled insults at Jesus.' *(Mark 15:29)*

- A sacrificial post is essential: 'Never do they immolate an animal without a sacrificial post.' *(Sathapatha Brahmana 3.7.3.1)* The post to which Christ was attached was cross-shaped. 'He went out carrying his cross, and came to 'The Place of the Skull' as it is called... There they crucified him.' *(John 19:17,18)*

- The victim is rejected by all: 'The sacrificial animal should be rejected by its father, mother, brother, sister and friends.' *(Itareya Brahmana 2:16)* 'He was despised and rejected by men...' *(Isaiah 53:3)*

- The victim should be uncomplaining: 'Like a horse I have yoked myself - well knowing to the pole. I seek neither release nor turning back.' *(Rig Veda 5:46.1)* He was oppressed and afflicted, yet He did not open His mouth; He was led like a lamb to the slaughter.' *(Isaiah 53:7)*

When sacrificing, the Vedic ritual entailed the sacrificer 'buying back' or 'redeeming' the valuable items of the sacrifice, by replacing them with more expendable, cheaper ones! In Christ's sacrifice, he bought back the eternal destinies of those for whom his sacrifice is effective - all his followers throughout all time and space - subverting the ritual to his own cosmic ends with his redeeming love *by replacing the tarnished and sinful souls of his own followers with his own sinless perfection.*

Every Hindu knows that a sacrifice can only be made through a priest, the worshipper cannot do it himself, but has to pay a priest to do it; and the effectiveness of the sacrifice depends in large part on how good the priest is! He stands in the sinner's place, answering and atoning for any charge of sin, by paying the full penalty on the worshipper's behalf. As the high priest, Jesus stands in place of the sacrificer before his own father *nirguna brahman*, so the most high God sees - not a sinful person offering a sacrifice - but his own pure and sinless son. *Here is a sacrifice that cannot possibly fail!*

From Shadow to Light

Acharya Prakash describes the Lord Jesus Christ as 'the fulfillment of the Vedic quest'. In him, many of the metaphors found in the Vedas have their literal as well as their allegorical fulfillment. 'Apart from the fact of the Incarnation of Christ in history, the Prajapati (the creator God) is not yet known... The avatara corresponding to the description of the Saguna Jesus is not yet revealed. The *Nishkalanka* (sinless one) is still looked for.'

Christ was a good karma yogic, which is good news for any western Asian who might want to follow this God-Man of mythology and history alike, who has won the west by his matchless teaching, selfless life and undying love. Yet his priestly role is sufficiently Asian that becoming his disciple does not have to mean the complete abandonment of Asian concepts of spirituality. Many have found that following Christ is not a repudiation, but a *fulfillment* of Asian spirituality.

One who found this out for himself was Shailendra Singh, a college professor in Agra: 'Christ's life was offered as a perfect sacrifice. I strongly believe that when Hindus are offering sacrifices at religious ceremonies, these sacrifices are merely a shadow of the death of Christ. Geographically, wherever explorers have reached, they find a tradition of sacrificing - even in cultures that are geographically far apart. All seem to have a very old sacrificial tradition.

'I believe the Cain and Abel sacrifices described early on in the Bible are amongst the earliest. The first Hindus believed that sacrifice was the centre of the universe. The *Rig Veda* teaches that the whole world came from one Man who created the universe and everyone in it. That Man was killed from the beginning of creation, and all blessings flow from his death. Christians believe that Jesus was that Man.

'Animal sacrifices were popular originally, though now only grain is sacrificed. For eternal salvation, no lesser sacrifice than that of the creator himself - who came down in the person of Jesus - is adequate. His purpose in coming was to participate in a sacrifice that would lead to the redemption of every individual who believes on him.

'Sacrificial systems lay great emphasis on the need for every detail to be right - a perfect High Priest offering a perfect sacrifice. Every time a Hindu utters a *mantra* and makes his sacrifice, it is a shadow of Christ's sacrifice. Christ subverted the ritual, putting himself on the altar. There could be nothing more valuable in the whole universe than the creator himself.'

Some refining and reformation will be needed, but the word 'conversion' shouldn't enter the situation. Sunder Raj points out that, 'Christianity is about as ancient, eastern and indigenous to India as is any other faith.' Following Christ - who was a semitic Asian - is not a denial of Asian culture, but a positive affirmation of eastern tradition, that also affirms the western culture in which the immigrant finds him or herself transplanted.

'The raft of knowledge
ferries the worst sinner to safety.'
- Bhagavad Gita 4

JNANA YOGA: *What about gurus?*

It is a warm June evening in London. Outside the Royal Albert Hall a group of fundementalist Christians wave their banners and placades protesting about the event which is shortly to take place inside the hallowed building. Tonight, Sri Mataji Nirmala Devi is in town. An acclaimed *guru*, she will explain how the obscure practice of *Sahaja Yoga* can unlock your full potential, and enable you to receive the tangible experience of your inner self.

Inside the venue, a full programme of Indian music is underway. Sitar, tablas, harmonium, sarod and dilruba weave their exotic spell, evoking warm nights of eastern promise beside the balmy Ganges. Delicate melodies weave around the hollow rhythm of the tabla drums. But no sign of Sri Mataji.

Next, an academic appears to explain what will shortly take place. An accomplished warm-up man, he explains that the end of the millenium will be 'wake up time'. In a busy age, it is important to pause and ask what it is that we are being busy about. Still no Sri Mataji.

There are escape routes, we are told; but escape from what? There will be guides and teachers, but can they deliver the goods or not? There will be many false teachers, and the commodity of common sense is needed to distinguish them. Power, money and sex are the keys to lack of sincerity.

Then suddenly, there is stirring in the half-full hall, particularly amongst the 65-70% who are of Asian extraction, in all shapes, sizes and ages. An elderly woman has appeared on stage, and hands reach out to her. Two small children present her with flowers, and are allowed to plant kisses upon her cheeks. Sri Mataji has arrived and, nearly two hours into proceedings, the evening has moved up a gear.

The warm-up man speaks more confidently now, platitudes dropping from his lips: 'Women should not be treated as consumer objects'; 'There needs to be a sun to have sunshine, but without sunshine, who would know that there was a sun?' He speaks of 'a festival of becoming'; he claims that kundalini energy is the same as the Holy Spirit, without any kind of explanation as to how this wild conclusion has been arrived at! 'Taste the food and know the cook,' he says, but we have yet to taste the guru's cooking.

Some blurred, out-of-focus snapshots are projected. Those are waves of kundalini energy radiating around Sri Mataji in this photo, he says. But the photos might be fakes. She's sitting there now; if she can really produce those effects, let's see them *now* rather than in these old photographs! Why, those 'balls of radiance' look more like light getting into the camera than a physical phenomena that was present when the shots were taken...

'Truth is what it is,' Sri Mataji says, speaking clearly, without notes. 'It is impossible for seers and prophets to explain.' Then there are going to be many disappointed people here, who have come specifically to hear her explanation! She laments that there are many who seek to make money in the name of God; at least she is not charging people to hear her tonight.

'You are true spirit. There is an all pervading power of divine love. It is so simple that people don't understand it. You are the source of all joy and knowledge; that is what you are, for free. You must honour and respect yourselves; I can't understand why people in the west go around feeling guilty all the time.' She sees religion as simply 'something you are born into.'

'I can't force anyone,' she says. 'If you want to go to heaven, then go to heaven. If you want to go to hell, then go.' Some of us might be more interested in going to get something to quench our thirst on this evening that has been dry in more ways than one. As she begins to lead her audience in a meditation, some of us begin to leave. 'Take off your shoes. Don't feel guilty. Forgive everyone,' are the echos in our ears as we step into the warm night air.

It has been a typical example of a guru at work; no better or worse than the thousands of others.

The Modern Perspective

Almost every Hindu family has its own stories about the gurus. Family members have seen miracles that they have attributed to their personal guru. Disciples are encouraged to follow blindly and to worship them as god on earth. Their every word is taken to be sacrosanct.

In an age when the priestly rituals have lost their savour for many Asians, some are converting to other faiths - particularly a superficial, westernised form of Buddhism - while others choose to follow an earthy leader. It's easier for people to follow gurus because it is culturally acceptable. It involves a set of 'dos' and 'don'ts' so it's easy to follow.

You don't have to believe in a transcendent God, *nirguna brahman*, full of virtue, but impossibly distant. Even Isvara cannot be seen in person - unlike in the days of Christ - but the guru is someone they can go and visit, in his Indian ashram. They can have his *darshan*, the sight of him which is a ritual in itself, touch his feet in *perey pao*, and perform *sheva* or good deeds for him.

These deeds may sometimes seem a little crazy. Devotees will carry kilos of cement on their heads from one part of a building to another for him; this gives you a great uplift (as well as a flat head!) *Mitti seva* entails carrying mud from one place to another, to make you sweat. Sleeping frugally on ashram floors with meagre facilities make the disciples feel that they're really 'roughing it' and such mortification of the flesh must surely be good for the soul, they say. They can sit at their guru's feet and hear his discourses every evening.

Plane loads converge from all over the world. As the groups from here there and everywhere come together, the guru's followers can enjoy fellowship in numbers. It's almost like a pilgrimage. The gurus make overseas visits, a bit like missionaries. It's a privilege to have a guru in your home, though they always seem to stay with the rich! Many gurus feed from silver plates, being waited upon. Ask them a simple question and you will get a dignified response; but don't ask them anything too complicated because they tire easily.

Lengthy discourses are the norm. Three hours or more is not unusual. Like Indian films that can be very long, people want value for money. Time keeping is not seen as a virtue, and long length makes up for occasional rambling; never mind the quality, feel the width! If the meeting goes on after midnight, it's even better value for money. Special mantras, instruction and counselling are given privately, one to one.

The gurus have representatives in many countries, with co-ordinators that keep followers in regular touch, almost like a fan club. Publishing in India is very cheap, so the gurus write in voluminous quantities, which are sent out by the ton in order that their followers can have a full library of their guru's teachings. If it's in print, it must be good - so they worship it. These books often quote (or misquote) the Bible, frequently giving very unconventional interpretations.

The book *Light on Saint John* for example, by the late Maharaj Charan Singh, of Radha Soami Satsang Beas, claims that, 'At the time of creation, the Lord, in the form of light, entered within all of us. That Light of God is the life in every one of us.' A quick skim through the Bible quickly reveals that it was not as light but as breath that God entered into the first human, to bestow life; and that the event took place slightly later than 'the time of creation' when the universe came into being.

Asians share by example, and in India will take people along to hear their guru if they ask to see him. Many Hindus eventually turn to Buddhism because they feel that their gurus are very shallow. Only miracles can avoid the suspicion of charlatanism. Buddhism gets away from the caste system so people in India are converting to Buddhism by the hundreds of thousands, in order to avoid the caste system. It's in the interest of the brahmins to maintain this system, but the middle class Hindus are disgusted by it and express their feelings by turning away from their traditional Hindu faith.

The Historical Perspective

Though gurus are very much a part of today's religious scene, the idea of a religious figure who passes on knowledge rather than fulfilling an intercessory or priestly role is more than 2,500 years old. It emerged, perhaps, as a reaction to the powerful stranglehold which the brahmins previously held on Hindu faith. What better way of loosening the priests' grip on society than raise up rival 'holy men' who, instead of intoning words and incantations that meant nothing to the average Asian, actually taught the common people about life, death, faith, and how to address the most profound mysteries of existence. Who am I? Why am I here? Where am I going? Indian philosophy desires to realise the highest values in life.

The key feature of this form of Asian spirituality, known as *jnana yoga*, is the involvement of a spiritual teacher who has experienced the answers to these great questions and is able to convey them to the attentive pupil. Wisdom, or *jnana*, is frequently contrasted with *karma* in the *Bhagavad Gita*. The word *jnana* stems from the same root as the Greek word *gnosis*, and this form of intellectual faith has much in common with the Gnostic tradition that thrived during the Roman empire.

'Religion is not meant for the next world but this world itself. Hindu philosophy was concerned with knowledge, which meant a study of all material "image" in search of its relevance and meaning,' says Abhisheki in *Religion as Knowledge - the Hindu Concept*. 'On the basis of this philosophy the ancient Hindu thinkers worked out a practical and dynamic pattern of living based on a Law, Order and Work Ethic.'

'Jnana-yoga seeks to impress upon the seeker of perfection the need to understand the true nature of self in relation to God on the one hand, and the physical universe on the other,' according to Singh in *Atman and Moksha*. 'This discipline requires the seeker of truth to meditate upon the nature of the self as essentially spiritual.'

At that point in its history - around the sixth century BC - Hinduism was heavily influenced by the newer faiths of Buddhism and Jainism, both of which emerged in India, out of the hotbed of Asian spiritual thought.

'Buddhism and Jainism were not different from Vedic Hinduism, except in that they rejected the authority of the Vedas,' Abhisheki explains. 'They really reject the assumed authority of some to interpret the Vedas. In this they helped correct a society that sought to be led by "authority" of texts. The Buddha stressed on moral action and refrained from dwelling too much on metaphysics which was too obtuse for the common man...' All things over-emphasised or wrongly interpreted eventually lead to distortion.

Prabhu Guptara considers that Abhisheki's point only really applies to a later form of Hindu belief, once the ideas of Jainism and Buddhism had been fully absorbed: Buddhism and Jainism not only reject the *authority* of the Vedas, *they reject the texts of the Vedas themselves*. 'All Indian metaphysics starts with Jainism and Buddhism; there is little sign of metaphysics in the Vedas.'

In Jain philosophy, the living and non-living, by coming into contact with each other, forge certain energies which bring about birth, death, and various experiences of life. This process, Jains believe, can be halted by a course of discipline that will break the cycle and lead to salvation. The basic beliefs are as follows:

There is a living soul, and there is non-living matter. The two cause the cycle of birth, death and rebirth when they come into contact with each other. The fateful contact leads to the production of energy called *bandha* (bondage of soul). Systematic control of mental and physical activity can terminate the process. Existing energy can be exhausted through certain austerities. Salvation, or *moksha*, can be achieved.

'There are certain scholars who maintain the view that even the radical empiricism of Buddhism was only a new interpretation of the older Upanishadic theme,' says Singh. 'If the notion of the self, as the Upanishads so consistently declared, was beyond all forms of description, why not begin with the realm of experience which is describable in terms of its own laws and could then be the basis for our knowledge of what lies beyond it.' (We will come back to Buddhism in the next chapter.)

There are problems, of course, in verbalising these concepts when they reach too high a level of abstraction. It's all very well to say piously, '*self* can only be comprehended when one has emptied *oneself* of all that is not *self*', but this quickly results in a contradiction in terms. How can one empty 'oneself' of all that is not self, without first knowing who or what 'oneself' is in the first place!?

Gurus bridge the silence of atheism and the mere symbolism of the mystic, to give religion a human face. Sacred texts cannot be interrogated. They can be read and understood - or mis-read, mis-interpreted and mis-understood, because you can never give feed back to a mute manuscript: 'Is this right?' But a person can be quizzed, asked to explain further, or to clarify difficult points. A *guru*, it is claimed, has apprehended truth itself in some mystical way by transcending the everyday world and tuning in to an absolute reality. *It is this personal experience that makes a man into a guru.* A true guru, who can explain all the amazing complexities of the human condition is surely priceless beyond measure.

World of Gurus

In his magisterial look at the whole guru phenomena, *World of the Gurus*, Vishal Mangalwadi identifies several reasons for the current resurgence in the popularity of guruism. These include: a reaction to hollow materialism; erosion of religious authority; repressive puritanism in Indian society; frustration with futile reactionism; and disillusionment with barren rationalism.

Mystic silence is not satisfying enough, Mangalwadi recognises. 'Personality demands conceptualisation and verbalisation of experience. Those mystics who formulated metaphysical theories to explain and propagate their experiences become gurus. You cannot ask whether their theories are true. You just "believe" and by "faith" accept them. "But faith in what?" You may enquire. Well, faith in the guru himself. He is a "realized soul". He is on a transcendental plane, in touch with the infinite. He can serve lepers or feed his elephants chocolate or have sex with his male and female followers. But he cannot be judged - he is God! Infallible! Inscrutable! You simply bow before his mystique! Thou shalt not think, but believe what the guru says!'

Many gurus base their astonishing claims on a mystical experience of 'unity', which they believe qualifies them to impart the saving word - the *deeksha samskara*. But there is no guarantee that such unity was the 'oneness with God' which they imply. Indeed, imperfect mortals becoming merged with the perfection of the divinity would surely corrupt God's purity and holiness, as we have considered earlier.

If a follower has doubts, such as 'If the gurus are all God, how come they often disagree with one another?' such thoughts must be kept to oneself. The trouble with a non-rational way to a knowledge of truth is that there are an infinite number of non-rational ways, leading to an infinite number of 'truths'! Truth ain't what it used to be...

Karma Cola

A young western woman visiting India was accosted by a man clothed in saffron, who offered to be her mentor. Like thousands of other westerners, she was in India seeking 'enlightenment', so this opportunity seemed too good to miss. Her 'spiritual teacher' led her to a cave in the Himalayas where other gurus greeted her and gave her food.

The food was laced with drugs. For several weeks, the gurus abused her and kept her as their sex slave. She escaped and returned to her native USA, where the authorities disbelieved her story and incarcerated her in a home for the insane.

Years later, she is gradually recovering, and has even regained her sense of humour: 'I should never have trusted gurus who wore

Adidas training shoes!' she laughs.

The story is not untypical of many westerners who have turned their back on the commercialism of the west and gone to the mystic east in search of truth, meaning and reality - only to discover people there who are prepared to commercialise and market those commodities as surely as baked beans are marketed in the west.

First there were the hippies with their kaftans and flared trousers, but pilgrims now come in all shapes and sizes from all over the west; as many as 250,000 from France alone are on the sub-continent and a good eighty percent are 'in pursuit of either mind expansion or obscure salvations'. Often their 'search for self' is aided by mind-shattering opiates. In her hilarious account of these denim-clad would-be sanyassins, *Karma Cola*, Gita Mehta makes the following observation:

'Who can deny that this is indeed the age of speed if the psychedelic escapisms, the mindless pursuit of chemical and religious narcosis, the greed for supernatural powers which entered our existence with all the playfulness of a poodle only three decades ago have already turned into a Faustian nightmare in which fundamentalist priests become bounty hunters, drug barons hold whole nations to ransom and saffron-robed holy men now deal in arms? And could the vague spiritual longings of those recent times undergo such rapid metamorphosis unless assisted by that powerful alchemy that turns doubt into certainty, the illusion of imminent paradise promised by marketing?'

The land of patchouli oil and snake charmers, elephants and butterfat lamps, where gentlemen of the empire left their visiting cards, now acts as a magnet for anyone in search of spiritual 'kicks'. Gurus are springing up everywhere to relieve the unwary of their innocence - and their money! - along with their ignorance. There's one guru, for example, whose urine is said to change daily into scented rosewater, which his followers are expected to drink! Is *karma* all it cracked up to be?

German seekers of truth are said to go to the Himalayas where they try to become supermen. The French are after aesthetics and the British, with a touch of the sun, seem keen to salve their consciences of the guilt they feel about their colonial forebears. Those are the cultural cliches, anyway! They don't want mother Mary; they want Kali, with her garland of skulls, drinking blood. As Mehta says,'The burgundy robes of a cardinal are less interesting than the saffron clad sadhu'.

Now in India, would-be pilgrims jostle with courtesans and

sages around exotic temples infested with large velvety bats, while
ISKCON devotees wander about, blitzed out of their skulls on
33,000 repetitions of the *Hari Krishna mantra*. It is a land where
stolen passports finance the drug trade; and a quick buck can be
made by fishing partly-burnt corpses out of the Ganges, and selling
the skeletons to western medical schools. These are the colours of
modern India.

On the river banks, mourners are haggling with priests over the
cost of reading each Sanskrit verse over a relative's funeral pyre,
while corpse carriers bring on their further cargos of death, and all
around is the chanting *Ram Nam Satya Hai* - the name of God is
truth - the traditional funeral dirge. The taxi drivers career about
like madmen and, karmically-speaking, it is bad practice to steal
someone else's parking space. There are more 'cowboys' than
Indians in India.

The west is no better. Krishna has become a doe-eyed pin-up
whose name has been taken for a vegetarian restaurant in east
London. Asians and Europeans alike frequently seek out gurus for
the 'quick fix'; they are looking for spiritual peace (*shanti*) with a
designer label.

The need for knowledge - and often secret knowledge - makes a
living guru all but indispensible for many people. Though, of
course, **Karma 'n' Chips** may give away many of their secrets and
erode much of their mystique!

Sat Guru, Is it True?

'I was born into the Radha Soami association,' explains a
devotee in Northern India, whose father and grandfather are also
followers. 'We have a living guru who chooses the path for
meditation. Previously Hindus had to leave for the mountains and
renounce everything. Now we can continue with daily life and
devote time each day for meditation,' he says about the benefit he
sees with the guru movement. But when pressed for tests
which will show that the guru is a true teacher, a *sat guru*, the
devotee replies, 'I am too young to know about proofs, but older
people who have followed the guru for many years have
derived satisfaction.'

When one of the authors visited the Radha Soami ashram in
Beas, he was appalled to discover the place alive with giant ants,
lizards, crickets and stag beetles. A shanty town tucked around the

back with living conditions as poor as anywhere else in India - only a stone's throw from a propane gas store and an electricity generating plant - was a disaster waiting to happen. Women and children were working on a veritable 'chain gang' breaking up bricks and stones to use as building materials. Nowhere was there much sign of individual freedom.

How do you know which guru to follow? For many Hindus, there are so many charlatans around that only miracles performed by a guru will convince devotees of his genuineness. But even the most popular of the 'miracle' gurus - Sathya Sai Baba - has been caught out in slight of hand. Prime Minister Narasimha Rao was delighted when Sai Baba materialised a gold watch for him out of thin air. The Indian state television camera team were even more delighted when slow-motion replay of their footage of the event revealed that the 'materialisation' was nothing more than a tawdry trick.

Devotees of the Calcutta holy man Balak Brahmachari claimed that his death was no more than a 'trance' from which he would awaken. They refused to burn the mouldering corpse, even when the smell began to attract complaints from neighbours. Two months later, more than 200 people were injured in the violent clash when police arrived to dispose of the stinking body, before the holy man could 'return from his astral travel'.

Bhagwan Shree 'Osho' Rajneesh was cremated with indecent haste after his death - said to be from an AIDS-related illness - apparent so that no one would be able to uncover the real cause of his demise. Life on his ashram goes on regardless, with video and audio tapes of his talks standing in for a live discourse at the atmospheric 'White Robe Brotherhood' meetings which close each day at the Pune ashram. His sustained appeal seems to lie in his unconventional approach to spirituality, communicated with pedantic slowness during his often-vulgar discourses. His undeniable talents as a psychoanalyst gave him a unique insight into the human condition, but most of his speculative philosophy needs to be taken with a large pinch of salt.

Super Consciousness?

What is the secret of these gurus' personal magnetism, and the extraordinary devotion they inspire? According to Bhagwan Sri 'Osho' Rajneesh, in his case it allegedly derives from a mystic experience in his youth, when 'another reality opened its door, another dimension became available. Suddenly it was all there, the other reality, the separate reality, the really Real, or whatever you want to call it - call it God, call it Truth, call it *dharma*, call it Tao, or whatever you will. It was nameless. But it was there - so opaque, so transparent, and yet so solid one could have touched it.'

It was a mystical experience of enlightenment, such as *tantrism* strives to achieve, yet one about which Tal Brooke says sardonically: 'Those who have seen the film *Invasion of the Body Snatchers* have an analogy by which to view Rajneesh's transformation... Something alien has taken residence inside the body and is now completely disguised.' Rajneesh claimed contact with 'the ascended masters', yet his behaviour - and the actions he inspires in his followers - seemed to many to owe more to Mein Kamp than to the Gita!

Sathya Sai Baba lays claim not simply to being a guru, but to divinity; he claims to be an *avatar*, an incarnation of God. Mind you, such a claim is becoming mandatory for any self-respecting guru who expects to be taken seriously in India these days. His flamboyant 'miracles' have earned him a sizable following; and, at least, he doesn't encourage sexual promiscuity or an unrestrained lifestyle - his theology is classic Hinduism.

Tal Brooke once held a privileged position in the inner circle of Sai Baba's devotees, and spent many hours in private discussion with the guru. According to Brooke, in 1940, when Sai Baba first became enlightened, he 'suddenly screamed violently and collapsed. His body became stiff, his breathing faint and he seemed unconscious.' Some would say that he had become fused with the ocean of being; sceptics maintain that he had become demonically possessed - or worse...

With another guru, Muktananda, it happened in 1947: 'I no longer had a will of my own... My fear increased every second... Then I saw strange creatures from six to fifty feet tall, neither demons nor demi-gods, but human in form, dancing naked, their mouths gaping open. Their screech was horrible and apocalyptic... An army of ghosts and demons surrounded me...' Another guru, Zippruana, who sat in a dung heap, explained to him that these visions were normal when receiving a 'blessing'.

Later Muktananda became fully 'enlightened'; he saw 'the earth being born and expanding from the Light of Consciousness,' and supposedly became a personification of the Hindu god Siva. For a god, he indulged in some very earthly pleasures, including tantric sex with many of his young female disciples. According to Brooke, many of the key disciples in his inner circle left when they discovered that he had been molesting a 13-year old girl.

Brooke said of Sai Baba, Rajneesh and Muktananda, they are 'possibly the most exclusive, powerful and secretive of inner-circles in existence. To get on the inside requires the most prized initiation conceivable. And only a fraction of humanity ever appears at that rarified journey in consciousness. The opening bid is to offer with total abandonment one's soul on the altar of oblivion. The goal is an explosion of super-consciousness beyond the point to no return. What emerges from the transformation is an Enlightened Master who claims to be nothing less than God using a physical body as a medium.' True or false? You pay your money and take your pick....

The Sanatana Sat Guru

How is it possible to spot a genuine spiritual teacher from a charlatan? What *really* makes a guru a guru? What qualities must a guru demonstrate? Many people follow a faith blindly without ever questioning 'why?' They adopt the guru of their parents, or follow the first one that comes along, without ever asking whether he is a false teacher or a true (*sat*) guru.

To follow the difficult *jnana* tradition - The Way of Knowledge - requires a worthy teacher, or *guru*. He must be a safe and secure pathway who is able to lead you faithfully through to *moksha*, or liberation. He needs to be a true and dependable teacher, because there is so much at stake. If your guru dies before he has led you through to complete liberation, you'll have unfortunately to start all over again with a fresh teacher, so it helps if your guru is also immortal!

Because he rose again from death - and proved this by appearing to his disciples on the third day after his agonising self-sacrifice - Jesus Christ lives forever as the eternal and true teacher or the *Sanatana Sat Guru* (The eternal true pathway). The Lord Jesus, who said '*I am the way, the truth and the life*', is the astounding fulfillment of the *jnana* tradition, many Asian Christians believe.

The forty-fourth verse of the *Gurugita* says 'The sound "gu" means darkness. "Ru" is told as light. No doubt, Guru is God who destroys the darkness of ignorance.' The Bible affirms that Christ alone 'has become wisdom from God...' (*1 Corinthians 1:30*) In him alone 'are hidden all the treasures of wisdom and knowledge.' *(Colossians 2:2,3)*

Adhishiktananda says: 'Christianity is essentially the handing down of a spiritual experience: the experience which Jesus Christ, the Man par excellence, had of God the Father and which He communicated with His apostles; and the experience which the apostles had of Jesus the God-Man, Redeemer of the world, who through his life-death-resurrection made all believers sharers of His Father's life and glory.'

Some will argue: 'Jesus is not physically there, whereas I can see and hear my spiritual teacher'; but the follower of Christ has the Holy Spirit, whom the Lord Jesus promised would be a comforter, teacher and guide:

'I will ask the Father, and he will give you another Counsellor to be with you forever - the Spirit of truth. the world cannot accept him, because it neither sees him nor knows him. But you know him, for he lives with you and will be with you. I will not leave you as orphans... If anyone loves me, he will obey my teaching. My father will love him, and we will come to him and make our home with him. He who does not love me will not obey my teaching. These words you hear are not my own; they belong to the father who sent me.' *(John 14:15-18,23,24)* All three persons of the triune God are involved.

A guru becomes a guru when he has the experience of being possessed by a spirit which comes upon him to qualify him for his life's work, but the followers of Christ claim to have the the Holy Spirit come upon them *personally*. Christ promised that his followers would be annointed, not by any old spirit, but by the same Spirit of grace and truth that participated in the divine act of creation! And it is a direct experience, not a second-hand phenomenon.

Seeking or following the *Sanatana Sat Guru*, co-eternal with the majestic and unsurpassable supreme God - must be done with great humility. Many Hindu families think that Asian Christians have become proud because they won't participate in any temple worship. Amongst westerners, the idea of someone finding something more fulfilling than temple worship, might lead to healthy debate with people competing to find the best way of getting close to God. But in Asian circles, this is sadly not the case. Change brings great anxiety and fear to Asian families, when it ought to bring promise, hope, potential and challenge.

The Narrow Gate

People are attracted to holy men, and listen to them, giving them a special status which often they have never claimed for themselves. Better to ask the guru some hard questions: 'audit' their belief systems to ascertain whether their claims are authentic. Christ is the teacher whom the other spiritual teachers hold in respect; he is the 'gold standard' - the eternal, true guide against which other gurus' claims must be judged.

When the great Oxbridge scholar C. S. Lewis was searching for a true faith espoused by a true teacher, he found that 'the question was no longer to find the one simply true religion among a thousand religions simply false. It was rather, "Where has religion reached its true maturity?"... Where was the thing full grown? Or where was the awakening? There were really only two answers possible: either in Hinduism or in Christianity. Everything else was either a preparation for, or else (in the French sense) a *vulgarisation* of these.'

C. S. Lewis was troubled with many of the unrefined pagan elements which exist in Hinduism, alongside the high ideals and wonderful philosophy; and also felt that it lacked the historic claims that Christianity has in abundance. In the end, it was incarnation of the *person of Jesus*, as recorded in the New Testament narratives, which swayed his heart and mind:

'If ever a myth had become fact, had become incarnated, it would be just like this. And nothing else in all literature was just like this. Myths were like it in one way. Histories were like it in another. But nothing was simply like it. And no person was like the person it depicted; as real, as recognisable, through all that depth of time... yet also numinous, lit by a light from beyond the world, a god. But if a god - we are no longer polytheists - then not a god, but God. *Here and here only in all time the myth must have become fact; the Word flesh; God, Man. This is not a "religion," not a "philosophy." It is the summing up and actuality of them all.'*

India's greatest gurus and holy men have some fine tributes to pay to Christ. 'The Religious Truth is found in Plato and the Upanishads. Its highest embodiment is in the life of Jesus,' said Radhakrishnan. Many gurus quote from the words of Jesus, particularly from his famous 'Sermon on the Mount', recorded in Matthew's Gospel. 'If I had to face only the Sermon on the Mount and my own interpretation of it,' said Gandhi, 'I should not hesitate to say, "O yes, I am a Christian." ' Here are a few verses from it:

'Ask and it will be given to you; seek and you will find; knock and the door will be opened to you. For everyone who asks receives; he who seeks finds; and to him who knocks, the door will be opened.' (*Matthew 7:7,8*) Would that all gurus could be relied upon to dispense such wonderful teaching, but finding a good teacher is like finding a narrow gate:

'Enter through the narrow gate. For wide is the gate and broad is the road that leads to destruction, and many enter through it. But small is the gate and narrow the road that leads to life, and only a few find it.' (*Matthew 7:13,14*)

Many have entered the narrow gate and turned their life around with a simple entreaty, spoken aloud or under the breath: 'Creator God, I confess my own sinfulness, and my need of your forgiveness. I want to live my life from now on as your true follower, trusting on the merits of your perfect sacrifice. I love you and want you to be my only true teacher, guide and *guru*, now and forever.' A new life with the *sanatana sat guru* begins as simply as this brief prayer, Christ's followers believe, though to continue will require the fellowship of other believers, and a thorough reading of the Bible - perhaps beginning with John's Gospel. *New life begins with this one small step.*

'Can you imagine how it feels to believe in Christ
and be so uncomfortable with Christianity?'
- Bono.

CHAPTER

8

BHAKTI YOGA: *How will devotion help me?*

A sweltering summer afternoon was drawing to its close, the heat relieved by a sudden shower, as Mike Fearon climbed out of the estate agent's car. His mundane flat hunting chore was also drawing to an end as he prepared to view his third property of the day. Only the estate agent's strange reluctance to come inside the ground floor flat - a 'Free Tibet' poster prominent in the window - alerted him that this east London flat would not be as conventional as others he had viewed.

The white girl who opened the door, her hair severely cropped, was friendly and polite. The vendor had just popped to the shop; 'Would you like a nice cup of tea while you wait in the lounge?' Yes please, he nodded, stepping through into a room which was strangely dark and cool. As his eyes adjusted to the dim light, he saw that the ceiling, wood floor and walls - except for a sunset mural at one end - were all painted deep blue.

The room was dominated by four ornate statues: Siddhartha Gautama (the Buddha) and his three identical brothers gazed inscrutably at him, as his eyes took in a scene which looked as though it belonged in an eastern temple!

Candles, bells, ornate bric-a-brac, incense burners, an imitation shrunken head and smaller statues seemed to be everywhere, with only the hi-fi equipment nesting on the scaffolding in the corner seeming at odds with the rest of the room.

'The owner is not by any chance from "abroad"?' Mike quizzed the girl.

'Oh no,' she replied, 'He's Newham born and bred; but he's heavily into Tantric Buddhism.'

Mythological Pornography

The word 'tantric' wouldn't mean much to most westerners, but millions of people in South Asia know exactly what tantrism means, and they avoid its practitioners like the plague.

'Tantrism is mythologised pornography,' Indian scholar Vishal Mangalwadi had explained at a meeting the previous year. 'It's an Indian philosophy which seeks to use sex as a gateway to spiritual experience.' In the west, this often finds expression in witchcraft where, in the Great Rite, priest and priestess copulate - symbolising the union of earth goddess and the horned god - Mike remembered, as the girl handed him his tea.

Tantrism has a right hand path and a left hand path. The left side is highly destructive, though it is mainly the right hand path which is practised in the west. Right hand tantrics interpret the sexual rites figuratively, while left hand tantrics - particularly in India - enact them literally, to the extent of living in graveyards, abducting children and engaging in human sacrifices. This is said to give tremendous psychic experiences and powerful visions.

When the flat owner returned a few minutes later, he was casually dressed, with his head completely shaved save for a long ponytail down the back; and not at all like a horror movie character. Friendly and helpful, this man from the mystic east - east of Stepney anyway - showed Mike the rest of his flat.

Was it imagination that the fitted double bed seemed so much like an altar? The double shower in the bathroom certainly had distinct bedroom connotations; It seemed certain that he didn't share a shower simply to scrub his partner's back.

Strangely, the most disturbing part of the flat was the one normally expected to be the most innocuous. The long passageway from the front door through to the back - obscurely lit by fluorescent lighting behind a dimly-translucent false ceiling - was like the entrance to a tomb. In the faint light that seemed to seep into the black-painted walls, could be made out a pair of bizarre paintings.

'This is the Taj Mahal, a symbol of love assaulted by the elements of earth, air, fire and water, but protected by the rainbow over it,' the host explained. 'The strange faces in the other picture represent fear, greed and other bad emotions.'

To most people, the second picture offered a completely different explanation. It was clearly a graveyard at night, and the dead had risen from their graves to indulge in some ghastly ceremony. It depicted left hand tantrism at its most grisly.

'It's odd, but the guy who painted these for me was a medium, and he kept saying, "Oh this is weird, I can see where the lines are before I draw them." '

Back in the lounge, the four Buddhas looked on serenely as Mike asked him whether he had ever been to the Glastonbury Festival. From his own visit the previous year, as part of a voluntary welfare team working there, many of the trappings of this flat would make it a des.res. for many of the festival's punters. Tarot readings, pagan rituals, witchcraft and the sale of occult items - including human skulls - are the norm on parts of the festival site. The two hosts affirmed that they had both been there, and were thinking of attending this year's event to run a clothing stall.

As he finished his cup of tea and the tantric couple began rolling reefers, Mike noticed that a small brazier had been lit in the fire place, but the room was still comfortably cool even with the temperature outside in the eighties. More disturbing, he noticed for the first time that the brazier stood upon what appeared to be part of a gravestone...

Yet the hosts were quite affable, and the conversation no stranger than one might have heard standing at the bar of any east end pub. They were selling up because they wanted to go to Spain together to set up a new home.

The scene owed more to The Addams Family than to anything more sinister. This man was certainly no mass murderer with bodies stashed away under the floor. 'Would you like to look under the floorboards?' he asked. 'I put this hardboard down myself. There's plenty of storage space underneath.'

The odd couple's guest took his leave, pondering the difficulty they would find trying to sell such an unconventional home in east London, even with the housing market starting to lift off again. Tens of thousands who flock to Glastonbury each year demonstrate there are many who have tired with conventional lifestyles and are eagerly looking for spiritual thrills, but some thrills - such as left hand tantrism - are actually life threatening. In their own ways, unconventional housekeeping and occult voyeurism are both risky businesses...

Mahayana Buddhism

Buddhism, of course, was founded by Siddhartha Gautama in the fifth century BC, and is seen historically as unorthodox by Hindus. In its earliest form - Theravada Buddhism, with its four noble truths and its eightfold path - was confined mainly to India and, aside from its denial of the authority of the Vedic tradition in both theory and practice, fits comfortably with much of the guru tradition of that age.

Around the time of Christ, a new concept entered Buddhism, effectively splitting the faith into two distinct camps: Theravada and its upstart brother Mahayana Buddhism. The former system was very much a religion of 'works and knowledge' with the individual expected to work out his or her own salvation in ways which virtually demanded retreat from the world into monastic orders to acquire the necessary wisdom. The latter system taught that merit could be acquired from compassionate being, bodhisattvas. Salvation could be made available not only to those who entered monastic orders but to all who trusted in someone who could take away their sins - a strongly Christian concept revolving around Christ who takes on the sin of the world, and bestows his own sinlessness in their place. In other words, it had become a religion of grace.

It rejected the emancipation from the world found in the Theravada system, seeing people as social animals celebrating a religion that was relevant to everyday life. Metaphysics, ritual and petitionary prayer were brought back into the picture, and many a blissful Buddhist began to worship the Buddha - burning incense before garlanded statues as a visual aid - much as practised by Hindus before the advent of Buddhism. Such devotional aids, of course, have been used since time immemorial in many cultures. The earliest reference in the Bible comes in Genesis 31:19, where devotional idols - though frowned upon - are referred to as 'household gods'.

A key Mahayana Buddhist text is the Lotus Sutra, composed around the time of Christ, which profoundly influenced the thirteenth century Japanese Buddhist Nichiren, whose teachings have recently come to the fore in Nichiren Shoshu Buddhism - perhaps the fastest growing 'brand' of Buddhism in the world today, though most Buddhists regard it as unorthodox.

The Lotus Sutra 'stresses the eternal Buddha-principle, represented in innumerable forms to work out the salvation of all suffering humanity,' explains Edward Rice in Eastern Definitions. 'In the Lotus Sutra, Buddha is the eternal, omniscient, omnipotent, creator-destroyer, re-creator of worlds - concepts borrowed from Hinduism and carried over into Mahayana Buddhism.'

Since the concept of salvation by grace arrived in Buddhism at about the same time that it arrived in Hinduism, around the time of Jesus Christ, the Lord Jesus was its most probable source. In Hindu thought, grace is bestowed by God, resulting from the selfless love for the devotees chosen deity. The follower centres his selfless devotion on a god or goddess - Vishnu (and his incarnations) Siva, and Ganesha are currently the most popular in India - often using an idol or image as an aid to concentration. This is called the bhakti tradition.

The Way of Devotion

'Bhakti is taken to mean constant endeavour to lose one's sense of estrangement and seek close affinity with God,' says Singh. 'It consists in loving meditation of all his divine attributes and glories, so as to qualify for his grace (prasada) and compassion (daya). When bhakti sprouts from deep religious conviction, the longing for God becomes an irresistible thirst for the vision of his divine form. The devotee passes every moment in unbearable agony because he has not been able to have a glimpse of his attributes in praise of which he sings and dances.' Phew!

Bhakti is puja, or devotion; it usually involves adoration and idol worship, though the 'idol' could be a living guru. You can sit lotused before the idol, chant a mantra and say your prayers; this provides a visible identity given to a formless spirit. It is easy to do, and satisfying for the devotee; it is more meaningful to the non-intellectual because it does not involve grappling with the unknown. The idol is present as a focus for singing, chanting, praying, dancing, ringing bells and playing instruments. You 'do your bhakti' and get it over with.

There is a parallel with, of all things, an exercise bicycle! Just as you have the bicycle in the corner of your room for a few minutes exercise each day to stay in physical shape; so you have a shrine in the other corner to stay in spiritual shape!

In unfurnished temples heavy with the scent of sandalwood, the priests will ensure that the idols, the garlands, the incense and other items are provided, and will help the worshipper with the ritual elements of his devotion. The worshipper may not have a clue what is going on, but they say 'God understands and that is all that matters.' Corporate worship provides a sense of community spirit, but there is no theological necessity - unlike in Christianity where Christ assured his followers that whenever they met together, he would be with them in spirit.

Krishnamurthy, in Essentials of Hinduism, recognises three stages of bhakti. The simplest is bahya bhakti, or external devotion, the adoration of something outside of ourselves, to be worshipped in a church, temple, shrine, or other specific location. Popular religion generally does not get past this first stage!

The second stage is ananya bhakti, worship of one's chosen deity within ones' heart. No longer idol worship, bhakti has here moved a step into abstraction, worshipping God without any visual prompt for remembrance. 'It clears the worshipper's mind of the cobwebs of superstition and gives a healthy direction to the spirit of devotion,' Krishnamurthy comments, though it is often at this intermediate stage that religious bigotry is found: I'll kill you if you don't accept my religion as the only true one! It is in this stage of fundamental zeal that supposedly spiritual people take the lead in the destruction of the mosques and sacred spaces of other religions, and commit actions which previously they would have been too disinterested to consider worth the effort...

The third stage, ekanta bhakti, passes beyond the naive fundamentalism and ruinous religious zeal, to recognise that for the truly spiritual and holy person, faith is worth dying for, but not worth killing or destroying for. As Gandhi said, 'To die in the act of killing is in essence to die defeated.'

In ekanta bhakti, the worshipper loves the blissful and eternal Lord for his own sake, not for the gift of salvation that is promised. It is the service of the Lord - an adoring service that implies centering the mind on him, expecting no gain either here or in the hereafter. It is a ceaseless striving for a constant flow of mind, brimming with love towards the Lord and his creation, without any selfish desire.

This mass devotional religion of heart is perhaps a more lasting contribution of Ramanuja's than his philosophical speculations. Though it can easily be practised by any individual within the privacy of his own home, bhakti has also given rise to many bhakti cults; currently the most famous of these, in the west, is the International Society for Krishna Consciousness - ISKCON, for short.

Hari Krishna

ISKCON bases its philosophy on the message of the Bhagavad Gita, as interpreted by the movement's founder, His Divine Grace A.C. Bhaktivedanta Swami Prabhupada, in his commentary Bhagavad Gita As It Is. Heretical by conventional Hindu standards, Prabhupada denied the conventional interpretation, that the 'hero' of the Gita was the reincarnation of the Hindu god Vishnu, claiming instead that Vishnu was the incarnation of Lord Krishna, who Prabhupada considered the ultimate god! The idea, originally proposed by Caitanya in the sixteenth century, served the purpose of revitalising a religion that was in danger of becoming strong on abstract philosophy and weak on devotion.

Prabhupada echoed Caitanya in the revolutionary thought that, as Krishna, the transcendent God could intimately commune with his followers. The idea seems suspiciously similar to the heart of the Christian message - that God is personally knowable, and lived amongst men in the person as Jesus Christ - with a few names changed. In practice, it is again a westernised form of bhakti, or 'The Way of Devotion'.

Devotion, in Hari Krishna temples, takes the form of rising at 3am to have a cold shower before washing and placing food in front of the garlanded temple idols; living an austere lifestyle; spending hours at a time chanting the Hari Krishna mantra (actually a 'hymn' of worship to Krishna); having marital relations no more than once per month, and then only for the purpose of procreation; and begging for funds on the streets. When one of the authors visited an ashram in Rishikesh, the sannyassins were engaged in a twenty-four hour continual chant of the eight-line mantra.

All in all, critics feel the Hari Krishna lifestyle tends to divorce the mind from reality, and to turn devotees into robots. Indeed, the authoritarian structure may fill a need for a disciplined lifestyle sought by some victims of the permissive age, while exotic and simplistic answers to questions framed and left unanswered by the vanities of modern technology and materialism may seem more satisfying than past pleasures of sensory gratification.

Krishna devotees are more active in combating social evils than orthodox Hindus; clearly the personal relationship that they crave with God motivates kindness to his creatures. Mike has personally witnessed the Krishna movement operating soup-runs in parallel to a number of Christian organisations for the down-and-outs who frequent London's Charing Cross and South Bank. It's unfortunate that their benevolence takes the form of providing high protein vegetarian meals for the homeless; it's a diet that produces rapid and severe bowel movements - particularly unfortunate for someone who, without a home, does not have a toilet at hand!

Practical Bhakti

This third major path to salvation in Hindu thought - the Way of Devotion - is the simplest and far away the most popular of the main paths, practised by Hindus in east and west, in simple villages and metropolitan cities. It can take many different forms depending on the wealth of a family, and the geographical location.

For example, when Ram Gidoomal's family lived in Kenya all the local Asians had brought their idols, images and pictures of Hindu gods over from India and installed them in their homes. Ram's folks lived in a fifteen bedroom flat and were able to designate one whole room as a Hindu shrine, a large and prominent room in which was set up a miniature temple. The holy books were kept there, with the depictions of deities gazing down upon them.

Every Hindu household customarily has a room or part of a room set aside for prayer and containing a shrine which may be no more than a shelf on which some flowers are arranged before a little figure or a postcard sized picture of a deity. In India, the shrine is often in the kitchen; this is convenient because purity is important both in the worship of the gods and the preparation of food. (All this may be obvious to most Asians, but for many westerners, it is a revelation!)

Each morning, with all the household present, the holy book - for Ram, the Bhagavad Gita and Guru Granth - would be opened up with great ritual. Other Asian families might revere different holy books, but typically they will begin the day with this ceremonial opening. In the early hours of the day, the 'gods' were woken with the lighting of a lamp, mantras or chants, and music.

Then the gods had to be washed and fed. This entailed bathing the idols in a milk solution every day, and covering them with a special cloth, a task performed by all the ladies of the household on a rota basis. In some households, the image is annointed with ghee, touched with coloured powders, hung with garlands, and offered flowers or leaves. Incense is burned in front of it and artee, the waving of lamps, is performed. In Ram's house, a special solution called tilak was made up, and each idol was touched in turn with it, on the forehead each morning as a sign of worship and obedience.

Before each meal, a portion of food was offered to each idol, and then distributed to the family and guests. All food prepared in the home was offered first to the idols or household gods. Prasad, food offered to idols, is cooked in a particularly clean manner, then dabbed on idols and pictures around the mouth. Fresh flowers were placed daily in the household temple, and at six o'clock dawn and dusk every day, Ram's family had a special devotional time.

The ladies would take turns to have a bath and then take devotions in the temple. This would entail sitting and reading from the holy books for a half hour or so at a certain time of each day. Would that Christians displayed such devotion! Sadly though, in many Hindu homes, such practices stem from a superstitious fear that something terrible might happen if the gods are not placated in this way. Religious ritual takes place often more out of fear than from genuine love or bhakti yoga, devotion to a particular god.

Many Christians find these Hindu practices completely alien. In fact, some forms of Christianity are nearly identical! Anyone who visits one of the Christian shrines in Israel, an Eastern Orthodox church, or many British Roman Catholic churches, will encounter a similar preponderance of 'stations of the cross', statues and icons, often with candles and incense lit in front of them!

Christian Influence

The key text for bhakti is the Bhagavad Gita. Lorinser, in 1869, wrote a metric version of the Gita and tried to demonstrate that the text betrayed a Christian influence drawing from the apostle Paul's writings.

Saint Thomas is traditionally believed to have visited India shortly after Christ's death. Very little is known for certain about Thomas apart from a few verses in the Gospels which show him in a remarkably bad light. In John's Gospel (11:16) when Christ announces that he will make the hazardous journey to Bethany, near Jerusalem where his enemies are gathered - in order to raise his friend Lazarus from the dead! - his disciples are incredulous. 'Then Thomas (called Didymus) said to the rest of the disciples, "Let us also go, that we may die with him." '

Thomas clearly had a problem with the idea of people coming back from the dead (and who wouldn't have a problem with such an idea!) When Christ himself was raised from death and appeared to his disciples from the other side of the grave, Thomas - who had not been present at the time - was sceptical, and took a very materialist attitude:

'When the other disciples told him that they had seen the Lord, he declared, "Unless I see the nail marks in his hands and put my finger where the nails were, and put my hand into his side, I will not believe it."

'A week later his disciples were in the house again, and Thomas was with them. Though the doors were locked, Jesus came and stood among them, and said, "Peace be with you!" Then he said to Thomas, "Put your finger here; see my hands. Reach out your hand and put it into my side. Stop doubting and believe."

'Thomas answered, "My Lord and my God!"

'Then Jesus told him, "Because you have seen me, you have believed; blessed are those who have not seen and yet have believed."' (John 20:25-29)

From the above, Thomas comes across as someone you and I wouldn't trust further than the local fish-and-chip shop, let alone entrust to evangelise the whole of India! Christ clearly had a divine insight into Thomas's potential. Tradition says that this apostle did indeed reach India, and died there as a martyr; there were regular trade routes between the middle east and several Asian locations that he is said to have visited, so this is far from being an unlikely proposition.

It is a firm belief of the Thomas Christians, the *Mar Thoma*, in South India even today that their church was founded by the apostle, who was killed around 72AD, though there is no record earlier than the third century that Thomas actually visited India. Europe knew nothing of these *Mar Thoma* until Vasco da Gama landed in 1498 and discovered a Christian community of some 30,000 families. It may be that Thomas's preaching influenced the final form of the Gita, with its message of salvation by grace through faith; though a Christian influence could also have spread through the numerous trade routes, just as Muslim influence spread several centuries later.

Because he lived humbly on earth as a peasant, *Saguna Brahman* knows all our weaknesses and temptations, and can identify with us completely. This makes his incarnation as Christ the ultimate bhakti deity, the God who truly loves us as we are, and who is supremely worthy of our love and devotion, say Asian Christians. Hindu deities help only their devotees, but Christ loves passionately even those who do not love him! He intervened in history to walk the earth as a poor man who befriended sinners, healed the sick, fed the hungry and comforted the brokenhearted, as a perfect role model for his devotees to follow, then he died and was raised again by nirguna brahman as the ultimate proof that he was indeed the perfect embodiment of the unseen God.

The Bible says: 'For God so loved the world that he gave his one and only son, that whosoever believes in him shall not perish but have eternal life. For God did not send his Son into the world to condemn the world, but to save the world through him.' (John 3:16,17)

In the Gita, Krishna says to Arjuna, 'All those who take refuge in me, whatever their birth, race, sex or caste, will attain the supreme goal... Therefore, having been born into this transient and forlorn world, give all your love to me. Fill your mind with me; love me; serve me; worship me always. Seeking me in your heart, you will at last be united with me.' (Gita 9:32-34)

This too, is the message of Christ, the true avatar of whom, it could be argued, Krishna is perhaps a mythological example. This promise is fulfilled perfectly in Christ. Lord Jesus told his disciples, 'Do not let your hearts be troubled. Trust in God, trust also in me. In my father's house there are many rooms; if it were not so, I would have told you. I am going to prepare a place for you... I will come back and take you to be with me that you may be where I am.' (John 14:1-3)

Krishna to Arjuna: 'Abandon all reliance on dharma and take your refuge alone in me. Do not worry, I shall release you from all your sins!'

With his sins forgiven, how can a person continue to carry a karmic debt? Like a condemned man who has been offered a free pardon and turns it down, not availing oneself of God's free gift is sheer stupidity! How can anyone be dim-witted enough to reject God's offer? Such a person has only himself to blame for lack of direction, in this life and the next...

A Relevant Faith

Churches in the east (apart from the Syrian church) are all based on the European pattern coming from Rome, for more than a thousand years the Church's spiritual home. This presents a profound cultural problem for the two-thirds of the world's population who live in Asia.

Though Christians in India are in a minority of thirty million, tens of millions of Hindus - while remaining attached to their ancestral faith - are deeply attracted to Christ, and do not hesitate to give him their entire devotion. Yet they will not enter a church building, fearing that it bears the stamp of a rival religion.

Asian followers of Christ who are not church members come into two categories: those who would like to join a church but are fearful of ostracism from family and friends, and those who simply find institutionalised Christianity unattractive and have no wish to be a part of it. Anyone who follows Christ is a member of the universal Church, the body of Christ on earth; but different followers relate to Christian groupings (or denominations as they are known) in different ways.

Swami Abhedananda has said, 'A Hindu distinguishes the religion of the churches from the religion of Jesus the Christ. The religion which is popularly known as Christianity should be called "Churchianity" in contradiction to that pure religion of the heart which is taught by Jesus and practiced by his disciples.'

Will the Church ever present Christ in sufficiently Indian clothing that the hesitancy in entering a church building will be overcome and those Hindus who wish to worship Christ as Lord can do so without fearing that they have overstepped some unseen cultural dividing line and compromised their Asian-ness? If that were possible, then a new form of Christianity would have to emerge - fully faithful to the Church's historical doctrines, yet compatible too with traditional Asian culture and lifestyle. 'The Hindu can accept Jesus Christ as God because Jesus revealed and lived a divine life,' says Kathleen Healy; the major divisions are cultural, and Asians and westerners alike must act together if the division is to be bridged. South Asian Concern is one organisation that is making headway in this area.

Healy, in Christ as Common Ground, has explored the values of Hinduism of which the Church stands in need, particularly the dimensions of inner spiritual experience and growth; but she also decries Hinduism's undesirable and unjust caste structures. If Hindus criticise Christians for being intolerant of other faiths, Christians can counter that Hinduism is intolerant of the inalienable human rights of others, who are oppressed by outdated caste structures. In their own ways, both faiths suffer from tunnel vision, oblivious to the cultures of others. But we mustn't simply walk away! For the sake of Asian families and children the world over, the problem needs to be solved, the nettle grasped.

Unfortunately, some Christians have a knack of getting right up people's noses! Too often, they give the impression that they know everything there is to know about the inexhaustible depth of God, when they know very little and resort to expressing themselves in a string of cliches. 'The blood of Christ,' and 'the power of the cross' are spoken of as though a couple of planks and a few pints of rhesus negative (or whatever was Christ's blood group) had any power of their own. They are potent symbols, but it is only the underlying truth that they signify which has any true power - not the outward physical manifestation.

Samartha in The Hindu Response to the Unbound Christ, notes: 'The scope of the saving work of Christ is larger than the redemption of individuals.' It was not merely an emergency measure or rescue operation triggered by the Fall of Man. The resurrection was not just a happy ending to an otherwise tragic story. The banal over-emphasis on original sin, stated in a crude manner, does not do justice to the full measure of God's work in every age and culture. It is that work, in its full enormity, that can and must be the basis for east-west spiritual understanding.

Christbakti

Many Christian missionaries sent to India to teach Christian doctrine were so fascinated by the high and lofty ideals of the Upanishads that they began to incorporate excerpts within their own services; the Church authorities feared the worst and compelled them to resign their posts! At least it was an attempt to make Christianity more applicable to the Indian culture. The other major step in linking eastern and western spirituality is through Christbakti - the worship of Christ within a Hindu framework, which is prevalent all across India.

Christabaktis sit on the floor instead of a pew; sing in Asian languages rather than English; instead of employing European hymn tunes, they use Indian tunes; instead of a church organ, native instruments are used. Is it all cultural window dressing? Perhaps; but even superficial matters can enable or hinder acceptance. Western trappings often invoke fear in the heart of many orthodox Hindus, and bring preconceived misconceptions into play. An Asian discovering Christ, challenges and threatens Asian society's norm: 'Isn't Vishnu good enough for him?' people will say. Often it is Asian women who are behind Christbakti, while the men are at best passive observers, being there, encouraging it and respecting it, because they think it might be good for their karma.

Christbakti has taken off because of its close parallels with other Hindu forms, even though it focuses on Christ, and the words used in liturgy are biblical. There is no shiva dancing or demonic praise, nor temple prostitution.

Millions of Hindus practise Christbakti - the culturally relevant worship of Christ - but view organised church groups as representing some irrelevant 'other faith', believing that Christ can be adored and venerated equally well within a Hindu framework. Yet the earthly disunity between Christbakti and traditional Christianity is not honouring to the God whom both claim to worship. Christbakti sometimes misses out on important parts of the total picture of Christianity, such as the Holy Spirit, and Christ's promised return to Earth at the end of the age, while Christianity often misses out on making itself culturally relevant to Asians.

What, for example, can Christian 'commitment through baptism' mean to an Indian Christian whose entire culture rejects the idea of changing one's dharma through conversion? But baptism should not be feared by anxious Hindus who see their relatives undergoing something which they see as a culturally inappropriate experience - the final parting point from Hinduism into Christianity. Hinduism knows the water sacrament (jala-samskara) that is not dissimilar to baptism, though it is seldom practised these days except in India's 'holy rivers'. From a truly Christian standpoint, Asians don't need to 'convert', but to embrace Christ within their own cultural tradition, looking to the Bible as their source of guidance and authority.

'A worn out, irrelevant stereotyped communication will not do. Christians must speak to listeners in words meaningful to them,' cries Healy in exasperation. Hinduism and Christianity need to meet at their highest common denominators, if meaningful discussion is to ensue. Purab ya Paschim - east or west - won't do; we need a spirituality which is appropriate for eastern and western culture.

India is a country crucial to the future of Christianity, but Christ's followers need to understand the diversities of peoples and culture, just as Peter was made to understand Cornelius in the book of Acts. The Christian needs to learn a new cultural and symbolic language in order not to give unnecessary offence.

'The Indian Christian today is enlightened by Hindus who accept Jesus Christ only to discover that their hospitality has been abused by the messengers of Christ,' says Healy. 'In order to embrace Christ, Hindus are sometimes asked to exclude their ancient faith, their tradition, their culture, their family, their caste, their inheritance!' Meanwhile, the Christian stubbornly refuses to change or exclude anything, believing that every aspect of his or her faith is authentic, when in fact much of it is culturally-determined baggage which is irrelevant to Asia and would be better being dumped!

One Indian Jesuit has commented, 'Jesus Christ has not yet taken out his naturalization papers in our country, but his application is on file!' Many Hindus recognise Christ as a man of the east; he does not come to India as a stranger. The stumbling block is the western clothing in which the Church has clad this supreme figure of bhakti devotion. But Christ himself has thrown off the western garb foisted upon him, and gone naked and barefoot to reach his 'sheep not of this fold'.

The assumed uniqueness of Christianity is an abhorrence to many Hindus; but the uniqueness of the person of Jesus Christ - divine beyond all knowing, worthy of every sacrifice, worshipped and adored through all eternity - is a radiant and compelling attraction to every human soul, Asian and western alike.

CHAPTER

9

YOGA:
Where will other spiritual paths lead me?

Academically, yoga is one of the six basic philosophical schools within Hinduism. Like the Vedanta school, it accepts the authority of the Vedas in theory, but unlike that school its practice is not based directly on them, but upon independent reasoning.

Yoga claims that the universe is composed of matter (*prakrti*) and of souls (*purusha*) and the soul is said to achieve liberation through the practice of yoga, because *yoga* purifies the consciousness so that the true nature of *purusha* becomes apparent. In practice, the word is often used in a much less precise manner!

The word 'yoga' is derived from two roots, *yujir* and *yuja* - the first meaning 'yoking' and the second meaning control of the senses. *Yoga* can mean a spiritual path leading to yoking or merging with God; or it can simply mean the mental discipline required to tread such a path. *Yoga*'s spiritual, mental and physical import cannot be separated from each other, claim the followers of this school. Generally speaking, *Yoga* concerns itself with *method*, and not with *theory*.

A *yogi* is usually regarded as simply someone who follows one of the paths said to lead to union with God. *Karma*, *jnana* and *bhakti* are the main yogas; some others are *tantric*, *raja* and *hatha yoga*. The various forms of *yoga* are not exclusive and most Hindus naturally practice several types of *yoga*, or pursue several spiritual paths - concurrently, intermittently, and with varying degrees of commitment.

Philosophically, the ultimate aim of the process is to dissociate ourselves from our feelings, thoughts, ideas and sensations; to learn that there are extraneous associations, foreign to the nature of the *atman*, but adhering to it almost inseparably so that the true *atman* cannot be perceived as a separate and independent entity.

There are four virtues which a good yogi is expected to possess: universal friendship (*maitri*) compassion for sufferers (*karuna*) sympathy for the failings of others (*apeksha*) and joy for the happiness of others (*mudita*). All are commendable attributes.

World of Yoga

From around 700 BC, Asians began to practise mental discipline, and the most celebrated exponent was Patanjali, said to have lived around the time of Christ - give or take a couple of hundred years. It was Patanjali who built upon the old *Sankhya* philosophy to add a theistic component, with belief in the personal God, Isvara. His *Yoga Sutras* had a profound effect on the development of *yoga*, advocating meditation techniques instead of the dependence on metaphysical knowledge (*jnana*) which was in vogue at the time. The mental and physical disciplines of the *Yoga Sutras* can be used with *bhakti*, *jnana* or any of the other spirirtual paths.

Control of breathing and posture are important in *yoga*, with the lotus posture being the most famous example. Jains, Buddhists and Moslim Sufis also consider *yoga* a good means of liberating the soul, and the Buddha is commonly depicted in the lotus position. Patanjali's system sought to achieve an extra-rational experience, or yogic state, beyond waking or dreaming; in other words, physical and mental yoga often aim to temporarily suspend the normal states of consciousness.

The expert techniques of *yoga* lead to the regularisation of all physical and mental activities. The realization of suprasensory perception is one of the stages of *yoga* training: 'This training aims at the direct experience of all things through identification with them,' says Yogi Kaul in *Yoga in Hindu Scriptures*. 'All the Vedic scriptures are considered to have originated through this process and it is, therefore, only in *yoga* that their key is to be found. *Yoga* is the guardian of Eternal Law, *Yoga* is the guardian of knowledge.'

It was once thought that self-mortification was a source of great power, by which any desire could be gained - though desire is itself undesirable for anyone truly seeking to get near to the supreme God! The power of physical endurance, or *tapas*, was considered sufficient to make any god grant a favour. Lying on a bed of nails is perhaps the most well-known example of *tapas*; though the most spectacular is burial alive:

In the nineteenth century, a yogi named Haridas put himself into a catatonic trance, and was buried alive for forty days, with a strict watch kept over the tomb. When exhumed, Haridas was unconscious, cold and rigid; but with the help of hot compresses, and artificial respiration, he was revived.

The Buddha emaciated himself for six years, almost to the point of death, before deciding that such self-mortification had no value. Only by recovering his health could he resist *Mara*, the Buddhist equivalent of *Satan*, the personal devil in Christianity, and by concentration attain highest wisdom. This is another area in which Hinduism and Buddhism differ.

The two faiths were perhaps closest in the era of Classical Hinduism, from about the time of Christ through to the seventh century. Here, when the *Puranas* were set down and the epics took their permanent shape, the three ways to reach God - *karma*, *jnana* and *bhakti* - had all become acceptable to orthodox Hinduism. What happened afterwards is a subject of conjecture.

There is a lot of confusion, with many contradictory theses, all of which seem to cast doubt on anyone who claims a definitive picture of the development of Hinduism over the last 1,500 years. That there can be so many different interpretations suggests that the view of Hinduism as commonly taught needs to be challenged.

Classical Hinduism is the last time that all the threads in Hinduism actually seemed to 'hang together'; to mix a few metaphors, the whole thing 'added up', and there was a definite picture there! Since then, Hinduism has been like a tampon or sponge that keeps absorbing without ever becoming saturated. The sponge needs to be wrung out and cleaned if it is to be a healthy container for spiritual exploration.

There needs to be a real attempt at reformation that will flush out all the issues. Because there are so few who read the sacred texts and really understand Hindu teaching, established thought patterns have become so engrained that they are difficult to challenge. Scholars can attempt tentative explanations, but these seldom filter through to the ordinary Hindu. A rough history of the more recent developments is as follows:

Religious Reformers

When the first Muslim invasion of India took place in 664 AD, it was neither the first nor the last invasion that would take place from the north west, entering along the fertile valley of the Ganges along the narrow strip of land bulwarked by the Himalayas and the desert. Life went on as the early Muslims settled reasonably peacefully at Sind.

Sankara cemented the foundations of Sectarian Hinduism with his *Advaita Vedanta*, its metaphysics identical to *Mahayana Buddhism*, but it nevertheless managed to see off the upstart faith: Buddhist worship was soon indistinguishable from the prevailing forms of Hinduism. By the tenth century, Buddhism in India had lost any distinctiveness and passed away from the land that gave it birth.

Ramanuja's theology gave the emerging *bhakti* cults a boost, particularly the *Vaishnavite* movement; but at the same time, Islamic influence in India was mounting. A decisive battle in 1192 allowed torrents of Turkish Muslims into India, and ushered in the era of Medieval Hinduism that perhaps reflects the faith's lowest ebb, politically at any rate. Spiritually, the resurgence of interest in *bhakti* had given it a powerful boost. In the sixteenth century, the Turkish Muslim's themselves fell to the sweeping Mogul hordes led by Babur, and his successor Akbar the Great - a somewhat unconventional Persian Muslim, and would-be religious reformer.

Though Islam had made considerable geographical headway down the sub-continent, theological compromises took place - in ways that have never been clearly understood - leading to a unique form of Islam unlike any found elsewhere in the world, one which genuinely sought to be culturally relevant. An attempt at complete synthesis took place as, in Amaury De Riencourt's words, Akbar tried to blend 'perhaps the two most completely different civilizations ever known to history.' His dream of a Neo-Indian culture, neither Muslim nor Hindu, was a dismal failure. A similar attempt at fusion, by Nanak (1469-1539) unwittingly led to the foundation of Sikhism instead!

At its heart, Sikhism is of course a monotheistic faith, with God as the supreme teacher or Guru. Sikhs believe that God has revealed himself to humanity and that his divine and creative word (*shabad*) came to mankind in a distinctive way through ten historic gurus. 'Guru' is also a term applied to both the sacred scriptures of the faith, the *Guru Granth Sahib*, and to the Sikh community itself.

Sikhism eventually became an ethnic religion, membership of the faith going hand-in-hand with living in that particular part of South Asia. Nanak repudiated the long-established caste system, and grafted Islamic ideals onto the Hindu system of salvation by works - *karma yoga*.

The next 'invaders' were the European Christians. Initially, there was no political danger from these missionaries who worked in India from 1579. Amongst them was the Italian Jesuit Roberto de Nobili (1577-1656) who, though uncompromising on doctrinal matters, allowed his high-caste converts to retain most of their Asian culture. Many eighteenth century missionaries were less tolerant; though few knew or understood the Vedic tradition, they condemned what they could not know and did not understand. William Carey was perhaps the most compassionate of the missionaries, helping to translate the Bible into Hindi, becoming a social reformer, pioneering the Indian printing industry, publishing great Indian religious classics, and helping people at a personal level, rather than simply seeing their souls as 'scalps to be won'.

Other missionaries, such as Alexander Duff (1806-78) chose a lamentably elitist approach, seeking to educate well-to-do Indians in the English language so that they could read the Bible in English! Still no real attempt was made to understand the *sanatana dharma* which reached England only in the nineteenth century. In one of Christianity's more shameful moments, the caste system was perpetuated, with separate churches for each caste.

Seeds of Renewal

'One of the main effects of missionary activity in India was, paradoxically enough, to help bring about a renewal in Hinduism,' says Brockington in *Hinduism and Christianity*. 'Efforts at converting Hindus into Christians tended to convert traditional Hindus into reformed Hindus, since the challenge poised by the missionaries prompted the Hindu intelligentsia to seek out again the resources of their own religion in the light of their new understanding of the past,' with the unwitting help of European orientalists, who made many Hindu texts available to the ordinary Hindu for the first time!

Theosophists and other western cults stole selectively from Hinduism, and misrepresented it in the process. The Advaita Vedanta tradition has come to be seen by most people in the west as the only 'orthodox' form of Hinduism. It isn't.

Many attempts were made to accommodate Christ's message within an Asian framework. Ram Mohan Roy worked closely with William Carey, seeking to strip Christianity of anything which would give unnecessary offence to Hindus, keeping mainly just the moral precepts. Much misunderstood, he was unprepared for the uncharitable backlash he received from missionaries, for cutting away most of the cultural trappings of Christianity - both the original first century Jewish trappings, and the European trappings acquired in transmission. Inevitably he removed much of the 'historical Christ', on the grounds that India already had a wonder-working pantheon, and he did not wish to see Jesus merely added to the list, but too little was retained for the faith to remain authentic.

Hindu reform, particularly of social customs, gained considerable momentum in the early nineteenth century, leading to Modern Hinduism. Ram Mohan Roy was a significant reformer, helping to bring about the abolition in 1829 of *sati* - the practice of burning widows on their husband's funeral pyre. Further reform is much overdue: An ominous sign of the times in the 1990s is the dramatic rise in numbers both of young women being burnt to death by their husband's family, leaving him free to marry again and obtain another dowry, and of baby girls being murdered by their own parents because of their low perceived worth...

Swami Vivekananda, inaugurator of the Ramakrishna movement, maintained that the first five verses of John's Gospel contain the whole essence of Christianity. It's certainly very Asian in its thought forms. Unlike, say, Swami Akhilananda, Vivekananda never really understood the significance of Christ's atoning death - though he claimed he did - and never had a personal encounter with Jesus in all his fullness and power. Seeing Christ simply as another *avatar*, he attempted to fit Jesus into the *advaiata vedanta* tradition. Many consider that there is actually no room in *advaita* for *avatars*!

Gandhi, perhaps the most famous Hindu of the twentieth century, interpreted the Gita unusually, as commending calmness, generosity and selfless action in the midst of suffering - a standpoint which motivated him to campaign for the rights of others, to reject the caste system as a later accretion to Hindu faith, and to commend both the pursuit of truth, and non-violence seen as love in action: 'Jesus was the most active resister known perhaps to history. His was non-violence par excellence.'

The latter point has parallels for Christians who see Christ's redeeming death as being the ultimate expression of selfless love. Hinduism can contain a wide range of diverse beliefs - it is, indeed, more a culture than a creed - so that Gandhi's belief in truth and non-violence as pathways to God, sat comfortably amid the faith's other contradictions and paradoxims. Gandhi was fascinated by Christ, and his favourite hymn was *When I Survey the Wondrous Cross*, with its message of committed renunciation and self-giving even unto death:

> When I survey the wonderous cross
> On which the prince of glory died,
> My richest gain I count but loss,
> And pour contempt on all my pride.
>
> See from his hands, his side, his feet,
> Sorrow and love flow mingled down.
> Did err such love and sorrow meet,
> Or thorns compose so rich a crown?

According to Samartha in *The Hindu Response to the Unbound Christ*, 'Gandhi strongly emphasised over and over again that Christ and his teachings were not the possession of western Christianity and that to follow the example and teachings of Christ one need not leave one's community and culture... Gandhi totally rejected the assumption that only Christians within the hedge of the Church can "truly believe" in Christ and correctly interpret his teachings.'

Radhakrishnan (President of India 1962-67) accepted that Christ is an incarnation of God, giving form and expression to the dream which had haunted humanity for generations, but denied his uniqueness. 'Christ is not a datum of history, but a judgement of history. Jesus' insight is expressive of a timeless spiritual fact.'

Nehru, steeped in Indian history and culture, had a high regard for religious ideals like freedom, tolerance, truth, and unity in diversity. He saw the whole philosophy of the Upanishads as tending towards the softening of divisions, and the undermining of class hatreds.

Hinduism has been through many changes to emerge into the contemporary world with excessive historical baggage, and perhaps more cultural trappings than it can comfortably handle. It has accumulated ever more 'ways of reaching God', some of which seem to have been inadequately road tested...

The typical Asian's understanding of his own ancestral faith is often scrappy and sometimes contradictory. The non-Hindu frequently shares the same questions and perplexities. Many people experience such periods in their life when they feel that they are going around in circles like a ship whose rudder has stuck. This has led to India becoming, like most western countries, a land of confusion.

Still the spiritual search goes on. How about a shot of *tantrism*? Or *raja yoga*? Perhaps mixed with a pinch of *hatha yoga*? And don't forget the *dhyana yoga*, stuck like a cherry on the side! The impact of western lifestyle often seems to encourage a spiritual cocktail mentality.

Tantric Yoga

Tantrism is about debauchery and degradation, eating turds and handling corpses, in the belief that by destroying the last vestiges of decency and humanity, a person can become a channel for powerful occult forces. Historically, the rise of tantrism coincided with the ascent of Islamic and western influences - the degeneration of spiritual life spread to all the other areas of life.

'In India we are keen on defecation,' says Gita Mehta. 'As part of a general concern with purification which is tied up with recognising the body as the temple of the soul, phlegm and faeces have no place in a temple. The man who strains towards Nirvana must be sure to void his bowels regularly.'

'What isn't piety is apt to be indecency. What isn't metaphysics is intrigue,' E. M. Forster once said about modern India. It's true that anyone who, first thing of a morning, cannot take the sight of rows of men squatting over an open sewer relieving themselves of last night's chicken buna will not last long in an Indian city. Another bizarre exploit of yogins is to expel several feet of intestine for washing in warm saline solution; this is not for the faint-hearted. Sadly, concern for bodily purification does not extend to the street, where nauseating wastes ejected from the flesh are left to fester on the pavements...

Some consider that the sexual revolution in the west has accelerated sexual competition and increased the fear of impotence. Many gurus exhort their western disciples to overcome their phobias by acting out their sexual fantasies until they have all been exhausted.

Mehta recounts the story of the young American woman who misunderstood her guru's instructions that his disciples needed to love him in order to reach knowledge of his 'godhead'. She burst into his bedroom that night, crying 'Take me, lover! I'm yours!' The guru had her thrown out of the ashram, and surrounded himself with a veritable praetorian guard of wholesome young men, to keep any other randy young women at bay. The guru is now suspected of harbouring homosexual tendencies...

South Asia has finally discovered the so-called 'sexual revolution', and even the erotic 'anything-goes' mysticism of *tantric yoga* is teetering on the brink of acceptance. The rites and wrongs of tantrism are hotly debated, with a view to discovering whether sexual magic should be allowed to play a role in orthodox Hinduism, but Osho made it all passe anyway. The machismo of the 'mumbo' and the jubilance of the 'jumbo' are all forgotten as the would-be *sanyassins* get down and bonk like debauched rabbits. The weird and wonderful fantasies of tantrism's spiritual fascism allow you to be the victim and the victimised, winner and loser, without limitation or responsibility:

For example, a bizarre branch of *tantrism* in Nepal chooses five-year old girls to be symbols of the incarnate goddess, which they remain until they reach puberty. Thereafter a girl 'retires' on a lifetime's gratuity, which is immediately withdrawn should she ever lose her virginity. These 'pensioners' are jealously guarded and kept away from the opposite sex, because their 'pensions' are often the only income available to support the whole family.

Perhaps E. M. Forster was right...

Hatha Yoga

Hatha yoga primarily takes the form of physical exercises, putting the body through a torturous series of postures which are intended to lead to good physical health. It is said to make body fat more flexible; the internal organs are massaged; blood circulation is regulated; and the nerves are balanced. It's supposed to be a cathartic experience.

In ashrams across India, and even in the west these days, gurus routinely use *hatha yoga* as part of their program. The gurus and mystics regard it as a preparation for *raja yoga* - the royal road to enlightenment, though it has no discernable spiritual content. *Hatha yoga* is almost a secular version of Hinduism, though many of the names of the positions are those of Hindu gods; some believe that, in using these positions, one is worshipping the god after whom the position is named....

Many Hindus, but not all, consider that 'the supreme power of nature' *kundalini*, or the goddess *Shakti*, lies coiled at the base of the spine, and that the techniques of *hatha yoga* are intended to release her to rise up the spine to rejoin her consort Siva, exploding in the brain. The person who accomplishes this in his/her own body then possesses all occult powers, psychic abilities and, supposedly, sinless perfection. It sounds more like a horror story, or a 'video nasty'!

Hatha used to be very popular in the west, as a form of physical exercise, before it was largely superceded by aerobics; but few western Asians have gotten into it, leaving it mainly as a native western phenomena.

'Is *hatha yoga* okay?' is the concern of many people in the west who have heard of spiritual dangers that accompany it. It's true that some people have experienced feelings of oppression, and even symptoms of what has been called 'demonic posession' through most have not experienced any ill effects - and others have experienced the same symptoms without ever trying *hatha yoga*! Anyone using *hatha yoga* might be well advised to stop it at the first sign of any ill effects.

Swami Vishnudevananda is quoted as saying, 'Many people think that *hatha yoga* is merely physical exercise. But in reality there is no difference between *hatha yoga* and *raja yoga*.' Such deception, when uncovered, causes discontent amongst many people following the *yoga* traditions. Often though, the reasons for discontent are much more domestic:

Gita Mehta reports that there is dissent amongst the followers of many gurus: 'I left the ashram because it's all so corrupt; the guru never stops playing favourites'; 'There's more politics in one Indian ashram than in the whole of the western hemisphere'; 'The people who are rich get closer to the guru than those who are poor'; 'How come our guru's got a solid gold toilet seat? Does he shit gold or something?'

In the Mahabharata, even the great Pandavas discovered that, though they were only playing a game, the dice were loaded against them and the stakes were for real. Many other have gone the same way with false teachers and have lost everything.

Raja Yoga

The eight disciplines that Patanjali considered necessary in *yoga* were: restraint (*yama*); the observance of mental and physical purity (*niyama*); physical exercise (*asana*); breath control (*pranayama*); detachment from sensuality (*pratyahara*); concentration (*dharana*); and meditation (*dhyana*). Together, they are said to constitute the system known as *raja yoga*, the Royal Way. Patanjali admitted that he had invented nothing new; but his achievement was to advance a mystic tradition to the level of a system of philosophy.

Some critics have denounced *raja yoga* as nothing more than a mixture of magic and shamanistic practices. Pratima Bowes, for example, in *The Hindu Religious Tradition*, claims that *raja yoga*'s techniques 'exist on the fringes of the Hindu tradition, derived possibly from aboriginal spiritual values and appealing to little understood dark and subterranean forces within the human personality.' It is said to meet the needs of abnormal personalities for deviant behaviour under the guise of religion. Quite an indictment!

Raja yoga is very complicated, and where Hinduism has really reached a massive number of western converts and profoundly influenced western thought - and, particularly, the minds of young people - is through the many cults that have presented basic Hindu beliefs is a manner 'westernised' for easy consumption.

Take transcendental meditation (TM), for example. Its founder, Maharishi Mahesh Yogi, became an over-night celebrity in 1967 when for a few short months, the Beatles - then at the height of their acclaim, following the revolutionary *Sgt Pepper* album - temporarily became his disciples. The social pressure on young people lead many to join the Maharishi's movement, in much the same way that peer group pressure had led them to purchase cuban-heeled boots and Pierre Cardin jackets a few years earlier.

Transcendental meditation had become that year's trendy fashion accessory, albeit a short lived one, and a year later it was about as un-chic as velvet bell-bottoms and platform shoes were to become in the 1980's. 'He's a nice old chap, but we're not going out with him anymore,' said Paul McCartney. Homely old Ringo compared the Maharishi's ashram to a Butlins holiday camp - though the food was too spicy for his taste!

The Maharishi was himself originally a follower of Guru Dev - later immortalised in the refrain of John Lennon's song *Across the*

Universe, written before disillusionment set in - and who had popularised the most basic meditation technique stemming from a ninth century Hindu monastic tradition. After announcing in the late 1950's that his Spiritual Regeneration Movement would spread transcendental meditation (TM) across the globe, nothing much happened until the hippy movement came along.

When the hippies went away again, the Maharishi dropped his movement's religious terminology in favour of psychological and scientific language, changed its name to the *Science of Creative Intelligence*, set up centres worldwide, of which one of the largest is in Skelmersdale in the north of England, and even fielded several hundred candidates in the 1992 British General Election. Worldwide, he claims some three million practitioners.

Yet his true aim seems to be to take his followers surreptitiously along the Hindu 'Royal Way' (*raja yoga*) through meditative practices that are akin to the Hindu liturgical tradition, using *mantras* which, he claims, have no denotive meaning - but which are actually evoking the names of Hindu gods or, in the case of the mantra that Maharishi gave John Lennon "Jai Guru Dev Om", extolling the virtues of Maharishi's own dead teacher! Each meditator takes part in an initiation ceremony (though they are told they are only *observing* it rather than participating) in which offerings are placed on an altar dedicated to Guru Dev...

TM is a mish-mash of *bhakti*, *jnana*, *karma* and *dhyana* yogas, in designer clothing, served up under a thoroughly modern corporate identity. For many, *raja yoga* combines all the other paths, and is the most difficult route of all to follow.

Dhyana Yoga

Here is the 'posh' name for meditation! Advocating *dhyana yoga*, Dasgupta in *Hindu Mysticism* says: 'Practising meditation they realized that Being who is the self-luminous god without a second; who presides over all the causes beginning with time and ending with the individual soul; and who has been incomprehensible because of the limitations of their own intellect.'

English usage of the actual word 'meditation' is often lax, taking it to be synonymous with 'contemplation', which isn't quite what the Indian mystics had in mind. Their view was that it was a practice intended to improve self-awareness and well-being: through body posture, through intense concentration on a word, object or image - or by a detached focus on what is happening in the present moment.

Many people have experienced altered states of consciousness/awareness through the eastern forms of meditation. Some altered states have been benign, but they can often be terrifying. The effect seems to depend on the individual: some meditate and reach 'enlightened states', some meditate and don't get there at all, while others experience altered states without recourse to *dhyana yoga* - sometimes through drug abuse, or the so-called 'near death experience'...

There is an obvious warning that needs to be attached to *dhyana yoga*. What is it that you are focusing your mind upon? *Zen* aims to produce inner stillness by focusing the mind on nothingness; another modern option, quietism, a seventeenth century form of contemplative prayer, took the form of suppressing thought altogether. Meditating on a verse of scripture has been most helpful to many people, but in its more exotic forms, meditation can be a roller-coaster ride into the unknown, leading to states described as 'demonic possession', or produce mental instability or insanity. The *aim* of *dhyana yoga* is to reach the summit of Being, but you pay your money and take your chances!

There are many differing views about the usefulness of the various yogic methods. Sikhs for example are very negative about all yogic practices, and ritualism is either rejected or reinterpreted in different spiritual terms. *Hatha yoga* is condemned for its emphasis on body culture, and *raja yoga* is rejected for its emphasis on esoteric experiences and occult powers. For an orthodox Sikh, *tantric yoga*'s emphasis on sacrifices and debauchery is totally out-of-order!

Mix and Match

In practice, a member of a typical Hindu extended family in the west may well follow three or four different gurus, as well as indulging in a touch of *bhakti* and a spot of TM. With the Radha Soami guru, a disciple is expected to meditate for at least two or three hours per day, so that's a sizeable dose of *dhyana yoga* too: The guru's frequent answer to any problem is 'you haven't meditated enough'.

Every week there is a time of singing religious songs, celebration (*bhakti*) and perhaps a chance to imbibe knowledge from the guru (*jnana*) there is *hatha yoga* with the TM and the symbolic *karma yoga* principle dictating that charitable giving is a worthy action. It all adds up to a *pot pourri* religion with no delineation. Hindus typically take in a bit of everything; the paths all intermingle in the average Hindu's mind. If it moves, worship it!

Some British people are attracted to Asian spirirtuality - particularly the *bhakti* cults like ISKCON - and have begun worshipping in Asian ways. ISKCON devotees often dress more hindu that the Hindus, with their shaved head, the saffron robes and the bells, chanting the *Hari Krishna mantra* and pounding their drums on the streets of western cities. But what British Asian dresses up like that? The British Asian is getting more westernised by the minute and certainly doesn't want to walk around in saffron robes with a shaved head!

It's a two way interface. Some Asians are recognising many attractive aspects of western worship. Those standard trappings of Christianity, the 'quiet time' and the prayer meeting can be very meaningful to Asians searching for a deeper spirituality.

Christian Yoga

The 'quiet time' has caught on in a big way with evangelical Christians in the last thirty years or so. It comprises a time set aside during the day to be alone with God. Usually it's done each morning, but the time isn't important. About twenty minutes is probably the normal length. Typically, the quiet time begins with reading a portion of scripture - sometimes with short study notes to help to understand the full meaning. Then a few minutes will be spent meditating on the scripture and its meaning. Time will be spent just being open to omnipotent God, feeling his *shanti*, or peace. Christians often end with a time of prayer, not repeating any set form of liturgical prayer, but holding a conversation with the creator of the universe, asking his guidance and blessing through the day. Intercessory prayer may also take place, prayer for the needs of family, friends, workmates and even world situations.

Church prayer meetings are often a total revelation to many Asians, because of the way they focus on God in a very meaningful way. These meetings often begin with a reading from the Bible, though this is not strictly necessary. If there are more than about a dozen people present - and in some British churches there can be as many as 400 people present - the meeting may well break down into smaller groups, so each person has the opportunity to be involved personally.

Typically, each person in the group will share some of the concerns they feel, ask for prayer for particular situations in their own lives and decisions they have to make, and speak about problems faced by friends and family about which they would like the assembled group to speak with God. People take it in turns to pray, usually saying short crisp prayers in normal language. It is a conversation with the God who dwells in limitless bliss, but without any formalism. In some churches, one or more people may feel that God has said something back to them, a few words or a picture that they will share with the group.

Hindu worship is often very disorganised and many find Christian liturgy to be a splendidly structured way of worshipping. The orderly format is particularly appreciated by people from the professional and managerial spheres. Music with harmony and reverence can be very attractive, whether it is a choir singing to the accompaniment of an organ - or even a symphony orchestra in one central London church - or an informal setting with a couple of guitars and perhaps a flute or violin. *Bhakti* worship can get cacophonic and some expressions of *bhakti* - Siva dancing for example - can be the cultural equivalent of charismatic Christian raves!

There is, of course, little 'Gita study' in the formal sense; groups of Asians simply don't get together at the *mandir* or temple to read and talk about the meaning of passages from the Gita - though the Gita may well be read aloud without comment by a priest or head of household in an Asian home. They have found organised Bible study, as commonly practised in most western churches during the week, very attractive if done in the right way.

Typically, these begin with a short time of prayer; a passage of scripture is read, and someone who has prepared some notes in advance introduces the context and meaning of the Bible verses. Other people suggest what the words would have meant to the original readers 2,000 years ago, and what the implications are for the individual in today's world. Inevitably, people go away feeling that God has spoken to them through the words of scripture and the discussion that has ensued.

East Meets West

Hindu fellowship happens because Asians live in families, and there are inevitably frequent occasions during the week when family members sit around drinking beverages and chatting about the day. With Asian extended families breaking down in the west, and the trend towards smaller 'nuclear' families with just husband, wife and children under one roof - with aunts, uncles, brothers, sisters, mothers and fathers, in other houses scattered across the neighbourhood - it can become lonely for Asians unused to the sense of isolation.

This lack of fellowship has been redressed by many western Asians through getting involved in local church life, where the cultural differences are much less pronounced than on the sub-continent. Some Asians have become so acclimatised to western ways of doing things that it's now the church that seems normal and the temple or gurdwara that seems odd! Many Christians are trying to live the way Asians used to live. They constantly pop in and out of one another's rooms or houses to chat and share, or perhaps to eat together.

Ram and Mike know of many fellowships in Britain and abroad - 'alive' churches with names like Ichthus, Oasis and Pioneer - which function virtually as extended families, bestowing the kind of practical care, help, support and counselling to which Asians have become used. It is a sense of community upon which Asians cannot always depend from their own families, unless they are prepared to put up with criticism and hostility about their lifestyles, the clothes they wear and the way they bring up their children.

Naturally Asians want to keep on good terms with their parents and older relatives, but it can be a serious imposition when such contact makes severe demands on your own life. The Church is therefore becoming increasingly attractive to western Asians - specially when they are facing breakdown in understanding between first and second generation immigrants, and antagonism between Asian and western lifestyles that we explored in **Sari'n'Chips**, and which can so easily lead to suicides. It's important, of course, to choose the right church; and here South Asian Concern is a charitable organisation prepared to help and advise any Asian who writes to: PO Box 43, Sutton, Surrey SM2 5WL, Great Britain.

It's an opportunity for Christians, too, to demonstrate the practical difference that a living relationship with Jesus makes, by helping and caring for troubled Asians in need of love and fellowship. There's a myth in some Asian minds that westerners 'don't really have families', that they are self-centred; but Christians are happy to destroy the stereotype by offering brotherhood (and sisterhood!) networks and community living.

The Call of Isvara

There will be some Asian families for whom the thought of a son or daughter frequenting, of all places, *a church* is simply too much. This refuge from the cares and woes of strained family life, and sanctuary of spiritual fulfillment, will be misunderstood and resented, perhaps leading to further estrangement between family members. But there need be no anxiety amongst those who choose to seek Christ, the awesome *Saguna Brahman*, in their time of need.

Jesus, *Isvara*, promised: 'Everyone who has left houses or brothers or sisters or father or mother or children or fields for my sake will receive a hundred times as much and will inherit eternal life.' (*Matthew 19:29*) 'Whoever does the will of my father in heaven is my brother and sister and mother.' (*Matthew 12:50*) Many have found this to be true, such is the compassion and generosity of many true Christians!

Life in Christ is said to be the ultimate *yoga*. It offers all aspects of fellowship, a sense of purpose, the teaching of the *Sanatana Sat Guru*, and the opportunity for excellent scripture study, worship, devotion, community service, prayer and meditation. So many churches, particularly in big western cities are so cosmopolitan and cross-cultural that ethnic origin or family background make no difference at all, and no one who is a new seeker after spiritual truth will stand out as different. Everybody becomes a follower of Christ in the same way - by accepting Christ! - so what's the big deal about being Asian? All are genuinely one family in the Lord. All have entered a new culture - *Jesus culture* - and are no longer westerners or Asians.

'Jesus told his followers: 'Do not worry about your life, what you will eat; or about your body, what you will wear. Life is more than food, and the body more than clothes. Consider the ravens: They do not sow or reap, they have no store room or barn; yet

God feeds them. And how much more valuable are you than the birds! Who of you by worrying can add a single hour to his life.' (Luke *12:22-25*)

What couldn't be done in India is being achieved in the west, by Asian believers. The *bhakti* tradition is being wed to the Christian faith that had once been regarded as a 'white man's religion'. All along, it was as Asian as curry and chapatti! Not only the *bhakti* tradition has found fulfillment and been given new vigour in the west, but the *jnana yoga* and *karma yoga* traditions are being reinterpreted and absorbed too. Soon, the time will come to export it back to India...

PART THREE: THE ARROW FALLS

'I don't mind dying,
I just don't want to be there when it happens.'
- Woody Allen

CHAPTER

10

SAMSARA: *What happens when I die?*

So far, it seems as though the views of those people who propose that all religions are basically the same will hold true. The differences between Hindu and Christian beliefs can seem negligible, compared with the internal difference within the faiths themselves, caused by the rich diversity of understandings and interpretations that have been applied to them over the centuries.

That's not to say that the two faiths are even remotely similar in the way they work out in practice. Both faiths - but particularly Hinduism with its practical emphasis on activities which are not part of its doctrinal formulation - vary widely in their everyday application. The village Hindu in his native land is often far more superstitious and given to worship of exotic local deities - and minor deities like Ganesha and the Goddess - than is his westernised counterpart; and a world away from the conservative European Christian at his midweek Bible study!

If we are to believe Genesis 1-11, both faiths have a common ultimate origin in the relationship between God and the first tribes of humans. 'Whatever the historical facts that lie behind the stories of the early chapters of Genesis, we may ask whether there is some common historical background to all peoples,' muses Martin Goldsmith in *What About Other Faiths?* 'Is it possible that all have retained distant memories of early history, the Creation, the Fall and on to some scattering of peoples as pictured in the story of Babel?' (The Babel story seeks to explain the origins of diverse nations and languages.)

'Other nations practised sacrifices, but Israel alone stressed the sacrificial system as an expiation for moral sin leading to personal reconciliation and a new relationship with God,' says Goldsmith. This God promised to Abraham, the common father of Judaism, Christianity and Islam alike, that through him 'all the nations would be blessed.' In Isaiah 53:11, the *Torah* teaches that Isvara, as God's suffering servant, makes 'many to be called righteous', though the context makes it clear that this righteousness is conferred only upon those who trust in God's true 'servant', whom Christians consider to be Jesus, who was perfectly obedient to his Father. Goldsmith takes the party line that though faiths other than Christianity point to God, 'they always need some correction to compensate for the corruption of truth which inevitably accompanies human religion.'

When St Paul preached at Athens, to people who were unfamiliar with either Christ or the Jewish faith, he referred to an altar with an inscription 'To An Unknown God' and took the line that these people knew *of* God, but didn't know him personally; Paul's own role was to make the introduction. Christ's mission has universal significance, and he is not some local deity.

The dominant viewpoints that underlie the subtle theological interaction between religions are called *pluralism, exclusivism and inclusivism* - but the average Asian in a multi-cultural society is likely to encounter them in more down-to-earth forms as sheer religious dogma!

Nevertheless, many Hindus may wish to know the stand which these three views take about the ancestral Asian faiths. Here is what Christians say about Hindus when their backs are turned:

Hinduism Through Christian Eyes

John Hick's book *God Has Many Names* is a good representative of the *pluralist* position. To simplify a complex argument, he sees all paths as leading to the Supreme God, so it doesn't matter which one you choose. As long as you are sincere in what you believe you will get there in the end, say some; but this puts our own beliefs in the place of God's eternal decrees. We can end up placing our own opinions in the position of authority which should rightly be commanded by God's revelations.

The *pluralist* view surmises that everyone's opinion is as valid as the next person's and that there is no such thing as objective truth; all religious claims are merely relative. This is not only a tautology but is also logically inconsistent with itself; the statement 'there is no such thing as absolute truth', is itself an absolute truth! It's as well that there are logic problems with the argument: if it were valid, it means for example that Hitler's views were as valid as Mother Teresa's...

The *exclusive* approach basically says that only those who acknowledge Christ and totally surrender to the mercy of God, revealed in Christ, can receive God's salvation.

Under this Sword of Damacles - some Christians claim - Hindus cower amid the legion of lost souls damned for all eternity! Other Christians, such as the Dutch scholar Hendrik Kraemer, suggest that those who do not know Christ must be left to 'the wise mercy of God' and 'the mysterious workings of God's Spirit' - as though there were still some important revelation to come which is not currently found in scripture...

There are verses in the Judaeo-Christian scriptures which give a note of optimism: 'Will not the Judge of all the Earth do right?' (*Genesis 18:25*) But to accept that God will still find some way to save those who do not accept Christ as saviour is incompatible with a strict interpretation of the exclusive approach. It's a cop out for Christians, and offensive to Hindus.

The third *inclusive* view suggests that God's gracious saving presence can be found in non-Christian religions, while maintaining that Christ (*Isvara*) is the definitive and authoritative revelation of God.

Theologians like Karl Rahner wholeheartedly accept the pluralist idea that an all-loving God could not consign the majority of humankind to perdition, but maintain with the exclusivists that salvation comes only through faith in God through Christ. *Rahner argues that where God is present in other faiths, then the saving presence of Christ is there too, just as he was present in Yahweh during the Old Testament period.*

Rahner also argues - though somewhat condescendingly to a Hindu's ears - that a non-Christian who has accepted God's grace in the depth of his or her heart may be regarded as an 'anonymous Christian'. It is his contention that because of a person's transcendental orientation (their 'hunger for God') they will always be looking towards history to find the revelation of the mystery of being, which the Christian calls God. He sees the Church as a tangible sign of God's presence.

Margaret Wardell, in *Chapatis for Tea*, says: 'Such Christians believe that it is right to talk to people of other faiths about beliefs they have in common. But they omit any part of the Christian message they think might cause offence. They are usually happy to join in inter-faith services where worship follows this pattern. They say let Hindus follow their own faith. Hindus have their own gods, so let's evangelise only those people who don't have any god. Yet, if the early Christians hadn't introduced others to Christ two thousand years ago there might not be any Church today,' so this is a pretty stupid view for Christians to take!

Hindus often answer this troublesome question differently. They claim to be *inclusive*, and all embracing, opposing no other religious views except those (like Judaism, Christianity and Islam) which claim *exclusively* to be right. The trouble with this view is that it quickly reaches the point of absurdity, with pantheism - where anything and everything is seen as a god.

Sociologically, no two Hindus, even from the same community, will ever have the same views of Hindu faith or lifestyle. The levels of diversity can be bewildering. In some families, for example, the colour red is prohibited; but other families may regard red as a key and important colour. It can often seem that westerners are being 'stand-offish' when really they are simply baffled by the fascinating diversity of Asian culture!

Christians, even those who have learned a little about about Hinduism from books or academic lectures, will frequently find themselves focusing on aspects which are often of little importance or concern to the ordinary practising Hindus. Often they end up knowing information of which 95% of practising Hindus are ignorant, yet miss out on 95% of the vital material which is of crucial practical importance. This is a common source of misunderstanding and confusion.

An issue which all religions seek to address, which is of crucial importance to everyone regardless of their religious beliefs, is the question of what happens after death:

The Question of Survival

Here, the commonly-held secular view challenges Hindu and Christian viewpoints alike. Death is the greatestest leveller. Both faiths have a common enemy in secular materialism which says that people simply do not have souls or spirits that survive the grave; that the death of the body brings the extinction of the personality. Everything is lost, and nothing survives to be reborn or to go to heaven. Put bluntly: 'Life is a bitch, and then you die.' That's your lot!

The hetrodox *Charvaka* system is the only branch of Hindu thought that is totally materialistic in its outlook. The chief views of this school are: the universe itself is the only reality; consciousness is the product of material elements; the soul is simply the conscious body; and pleasure is the only purpose in life.

The vexing question of whether any element of the human personality survives death occupied the ancient Hindu philosophers for many centuries, as indicated in the Upanishads. Though some considered death to be the end, the consensus of opinion was that the *personality* survives intact.

It sometimes surprises many westerners that theistic Hindus generally believe in a literal Hell that is quite similar to the Christian conception. Hindus believe that the personality is not retained if the deceased should be unfortunate enough to end up there. Medieval Christians believed that personality was generally purged away after death, though such a heretical view has not been prevalent for more than four hundred years, and modern Christians lament that real suffering takes place to conscious personalities in that infernal abode, Hell.

Summarising the Hindu views, Sharma says: 'The consensus seemed to emerge in favour of survival, as is clear from the widespread acceptance of the doctrine of rebirth. But just as the Christian belief in resurrection became widespread without any clear recognition of the exact process involved, the widespread acceptance of rebirth in the Hindu world went hand in hand with a similar lack of exactitude about the mechanism.'

Before Christ, many Jews believed that the soul would survive death, but believed that it languished in a foreboding place of waiting, a kind of limbo state, prior to a judgement day. Divine judgement is feared, too, by Muslims who are anxious for the final fate of their souls; they think their good and bad deeds will be weighed on scales, with paradise or purgatory dependent on the outcome. Christians believe that those who have accepted Christ, and come under the protective shadow of his grace, will go to be with God forever, while those who have rejected God will be forever separated from him. *Briefly: the Jew hopes; the Muslim fears; and the Christian trusts.*

Sikhs, too, believe in survival, and a period of waiting before the final outcome of their lives will be revealed. Only modern secular materialism believes in the total annihilation of the personality upon death. Other faiths believe that how one has lived life will *eventually* decide the soul's final fate; *but where will you be one second after you have died?* No one seems to have a concrete answer! Some texts, such as Tibetan Buddhism's *Bardo Thosgrol*, claim to give detailed answers, but most agree that no one knows for sure.

The Psalmist pondered this great mystery when he asked of God: 'Do you show your wonders to the dead? Do those who are dead rise up and praise you? Is your love declared in the grave, your faithfulness in Destruction? Are your wonders known in the place of darkness, or your righteous deeds in the land of oblivion?' (*Psalm 88:11,12*)

If the soul survives, the question remains: where does it go, and what happens to it next?

In its basic form, *samsara* (pronounced 'samswahrah') is the popular Hindu belief that the souls of the dead come back to inhabit new bodies, and are re-born into the world time and time again, until the karmic debt has been repaid, and they can leave the earth for good, to be united with God. In the west, the view is called reincarnation.

There are many interpretations of *samsara* that are currently in vogue. Opinions differ as to how many times you will have to come back, and whether a human can be reincarnated as an animal. The basic claim remains the same however: *people live not once, but many times*.

There is much, though, that the priests cannot explain. Is reincarnation instant, like switching a television from one channel to another, or is there a period of waiting pending re-entry, like waiting for a train? Where does the soul go while it is anxiously waiting for rebirth? There is no consensus of agreement; indeed, there are three rival views with strong advocates amongst Hindus: a continued existence in a ghost-like state; a heaven and hell scenario similar to that of Christianity; and *moksha*, or liberation from earthly experience - a view we will consider in the next chapter.

Christianity and Samsara

We have looked at startling similarities between Hindu and Christian beliefs, but with this Hindu concept, we get down to the 'nitty gritty' *difference*, for the Bible teaches that people live *once* only, and are then judged for the way they have lived their *one* life.

There are no comebacks and no second chances. You get one shot, and you'd better give it your best, because that's all you're going to get!

Jesus said of John the Baptist, the cousin who had prepared the way for his earthly ministry; 'If you are willing to accept it, he is the Elijah who was to come. He who has ears, let him hear.' (*Matthew 11:14,15*) Some have taken this to mean that John the Baptist was the reincarnation of Elijah; though Elijah was also believed to have been taken into heaven alive, and will return to earth one day.

Elsewhere we read that, when the Baptist was asked bluntly whether he was Elijah, he firmly replied 'No'. (*John 1:21*) In this light, Christ's words must clearly be taken to mean that John was a prophet *like* Elijah - thought to have been the greatest of the prophets in the *Torah*. Christ called John a prophet, 'Yes, I tell you, and more than a prophet... I tell you the truth: Among those born of women there has not risen anyone greater than John the Baptist.' (*Matthew 11:9,11*) John the Baptist was Elijah in the sense that he was the greatest prophet up to that time, which is a long way from saying that he was the reincarnation of Elijah.

And what did this greatest of the prophets foretell that was greater than any of Elijah's pronouncements? John gave this testimony: 'I saw the Spirit come down from heaven as a dove and remain on him [Jesus]. I would not have known him, except that the one who sent me to baptise with water [God] told me, "The man on whom you see the Spirit come down and remain is he who will baptise with the Holy Spirit." I have seen this and I testify that this is the Son of God.' (*John 1:32-34*) Indeed, what greater prophetic utterance could there be than the correct identification of God's living Word, Isvara, *Saguna Brahman*, the only begotten 'Son' of *nirguna brahman*, true God in the flesh?

John the Baptist was not the reincarnation of Elijah. No, except for a few heretical sects that died out nearly 2,000 years ago, no orthodox Christian has ever accepted the doctrine of *samsara*. Reincarnation, or the transmigration of souls, cannot be reconciled with the frank teachings of Jesus. As the writer of the Bible book of *Hebrews* said: 'Man is destined to die once, and after that to face judgement.' (*Hebrews 9:27*) This belief that a person has one life only is common to Judaism, Christianity and Islam alike, and is thus the prevalent view of the majority of the world's population. Even at the risk of causing offence to Hindus, it is a point on which no compromise is possible for true adherents to those faiths. *Or is it?*

Three Views

Theologian John Hick has identified three versions of the *karma* and *samsara* concept. He calls them the popular conception, the Vedic conception and the demythologised interpretation.

The *popular* concept maintains that it is the Self or *paramatman* which transmigrates from body to body; the memories, bodily continuity and mental dispositions which make up the personality are not believed to remain intact. Hick argues that in such a model of reincarnation, nothing remains constant from life to life. This version can be compatible with Christianity in the sense that Christians also believe that the same Spirit of God breathes life into every person who has ever lived, and will go on to breathe life into other people when we are all dead. (The Spirit will, in fact, continue giving life to every living person on earth at every moment of every life; so this model of *samsara* makes no greater claim than that all human life is a continuing process.)

The *demythologized* version was originally suggested by J.C.Jennings and can be summarised as: 'a mythological expression of the fact that all our actions have effects upon some part of human community and have to be borne, for good or ill, by others in the future.' Jennings claimed that this was the Buddhist understanding of reincarnation, and that it treated life as an organic unity and preached collective *karma* - though this is a difficult position to sustain. Collective *karma* aside, this position does not contradict the Christian view. It's so waffly and imprecise, its meaning is so ambiguous, that it could concur with virtually *any* view!

The Vedic model proposes that, although we regard ourselves as a single entity, we all have three seperate bodies collapsed into one: the gross, subtle and causal bodies. From this viewpoint, the subtle and causal bodies together leave the gross, or physical, body at the time of death and move on to inhabit another gross body, formed in another womb. This version is totally incompatible with the profound teachings of Christ.

These then, are the different ways in which Hindus consider *samsara*, only one of which is hostile to Christian belief; but what is the basis for believing in rebirth at all? Let's look at what the ancient Hindu scriptures say:

The Vedic Tradition Revisited

What does the *Rig Veda* say about *samsara*? Commentators fight like cats and dogs to claim that their own interpretation is the correct one; but, try as they may, no one has ever managed to find any reference to *samsara* in the *Rig Veda* - it simply isn't there!

Instead, there are descriptions of heaven, 'a place where light is perpetual. It is a beautiful place where there is happiness, pleasure, joy and enlightenment.' *(9:113.7-11)* As Professor Zaehner explains, 'In the Rig Veda the soul of the dead is carried aloft by the fire-god, Agni, who consumes the material body at cremation, to the heavenly world where it deports itself with the gods in perfect, carefree bliss.' No *samsara* there.

Not everyone achieves such bliss, however. A 'place of blind darkness' is referred to in the *Rig Veda* as the ultimate destination of some wicked souls: a deep pit and a place of darkness, where the wicked fall down headlong. The *Brahmanas* introduce the notion of judgement following death. The deeds of the deceased are weighed in the balance and the dead are rewarded or punished according to the aptness or otherwise of their deeds performed in life; a concept similar to the one found in Islam. Still no *samsara*.

The *Katha Upanishad* describes death as offering two paths, the path of the good and the path of the pleasant. Yama, the god of death, explains that death is not the end, in profound disagreement with the secular materialism which is the common foe of all religions. Wherefore art thou, *samsara*?

We discovered earlier that, of the three views on *samsara*, only the Vedanta model was incompatible with Christianity: but then, it is also incompatable with more than a thousand years of Vedic tradition prior to the Upanishads!

Reincarnation makes its debut on the world's stage at the very end of the Upanishad period. According to Zaehner, it was not described in detail until the *Maitri Upanishad*, which he considers to be the most recent of all the main Upanishads. Hinduism had gotten along quite happily without the concept for the first two thousand years or so of its history...

The tiniest early mention of the transmigration dogma occurs circa 650BC in the *Brhadaranyaka Upanishad*: 'The souls of those who have lived lives in sacrifice, charity and austerity... pass to the world of the fathers, the paradise of Yama; thence, after a period of bliss, they go to the moon; from the moon they go to empty space, whence they pass to the air, and descend to Earth in the rain. There they become food... and are offered again in the altar of fire which is woman, while the unrighteous are reincarnated as worms, birds or insects.' A very crude, mythological forerunner of *samsara*.

Even after its appearance, not all *sruti* acknowledged the desirability or legitimacy of the concept, with its antiquarian space travel. The sage of the *Shvetashvatara Upanishad* says: 'I know this great person who resides beyond all darkness (of sin and ignorance) as bright as the sun. He who knows him escapes death and there is no other escape. There is nothing superior to Him, and there is nothing that is greater than Him, and there is nothing smaller than Him. He stands alone by Himself in the heavens unmoved like a tree, and yet the world is filled by this person.' So annihilation of the soul (and, presumably, rebirth!) could be avoided only by *knowing God*.

The *Svetasvataropanisad* affirms that there is 'the mighty Purusa of the colour of the sun beyond the darkness. Only in knowing Him does one pass over death. There is no other path leading to eternal life.'*(3:8)* 'One who knows this becomes able to reach the state of deathlessness. No other way is known for this,' says the commentary at the end of *Purusasukta*.

By the time of the *Bhagavad Gita*, we find Krishna saying confidently that all who follow the incarnation of the living God, and trust upon him, will never know rebirth. *Samsara* had already been superceded philosophically and theologically, within about seven centuries of its primitive conception. There is little basis in the Hindu scriptures, nor in the stunning epics which follow, which authenticate *samsara* as either a legitimate aspect of Hinduism, or as objective truth. If the concept had emerged only a hundred years later, it would have been too late to be regarded as *sruti*.

In practice, it is a very common belief amongst Hindus, though it makes no sense. One reason for its widespread propagation by the top castes was that it was a good way to justify their own power, and their exploitation of the powerless.

'Some sects usually considered Hindu do not subscribe to the doctrine of reincarnation, and some religions of Indian origin other than Hinduism, such as Buddhism and Jainism, do so,' affirms Arvind Sharma in *A Hindu Perspective on the Philosophy of Religion*.

The *Lingayats* (or *Vira-Saivas*) a twelfth century *bhakti* cult were the first since classical times to reject the doctrine of transmigration. The *mimamsa* philosophical system denied the dogma of *samsara* for more than a thousand years, and finally came to accept it only in the seventh century AD. Ram Mohan Roy, founder of the Brahmo Samaj sect, also rejected the concept of transmigration of souls.

In practice, many Hindus believe one thing and do another! In the ancient Vedic tradition, the spirits of the departed live in a shadow world similar in conception to the Hades of the Greeks, Sheol of the Jews and Pluto of the Romans. It was the eerie world of the ancestors, who required of their descendents regular oblations of food and drink. Typical Hindu families continue to offer food and drink to their forebears on a weekly or monthly basis, giving the ceremony great ritual and importance, even in the present day. As Chaudhuri points out in *Hinduism - A Religion to Live By*, 'No Hindu ever considers the question of how an ancestor of his who, after rebirth is leading a mundane life somewhere, could stand in need of food and water from him'!

Many Hindus are terrified of the *samsara* concept, fearful that they or their loved ones will return to earth as a loathsome creature. Rabindranath Maharaj devoutly worshipped his father's spirit everyday from his passing, anxiously waiting for some sign of the form into which his beloved parent had been reborn. Some of the deceased's ashes had been kept for an occult purpose: Kept on a tray in a locked room, they were scrutinised each morning for a tell-tail footprint which would reveal the new form in which the deceased had returned. To Maharaj's shame and terror, the footprint of a tiny bird was discovered in the ash one morning. His world was shattered by the unwarranted belief that his devout father had been reincarnated as a tiny bird...

'Words could not describe the consternation I felt,' he recalls in his autobiography, *Death of a Guru*. 'My small world was shattered... If he hadn't attained oneness with Brahman, then what hope was there for anyone else?' His father had spent the eight years prior to his unexpected death as an ascetic, with his hair down to the waist, and it had been Rabindranath's *dharma* to torch the pungent camphor cubes placed strategically amid the logs of the funeral pire, and offer his father's corpse as a sacrifice to the fire god, Agni.

His family were deeply superstitious. Rabi's grandfather was said to have sacrificed his first-born son as an offering to his favourite deity, in order to accumulate great wealth. Rabi's mother suffered from nightmares in which his grandfather's headless ghost returned to the family home, and Rabi feared that someone had stolen his grandfather's skull from the local cemetry, in order to gain control over the deceased's spirit. Later, Rabi achieved true *moksha* when he became a follower of Christ - and was released from the primitive superstitions that had blighted his life.

The Psychological Crux

Though it is an orphan with scant legitimate parentage in the sacred texts, cruel *samsara* has become a key foundation of the thinking of many Hindus. Without it, there is so much that cannot be explained for the Hindu, that he will usually feel at a complete loss. Only the Hindu who has become totally secularised would be willing to dismiss *samsara* out of hand.

The karmic law hands down a series of life sentences for wrong doing, and without *samsara* there seems to be neither judgement nor justice. Life would therefore seem purposeless; the universe without point or reason. Psychologically, people need to feel that there is a purpose for their existence. Once the *samsara* doctrine is removed, they are often bereft of meaning and of hope.

In a world that sometimes seemed to be void of justice or reckoning, the psalmist cried out to God for righteousness to reign: 'In his arrogance the wicked man hunts down the weak, who are caught in the schemes he devises. He boasts of the cravings of his heart; he blesses the greedy and reviles the Lord. In his pride the wicked does not seek him; in his thoughts there is no room for God... Arise, Lord! Lift up your hand, O God. Do not forget the helpless.' (Psalm 10:2-4,12)

If the wicked do not receive their just deserts in some future life, then how can God be just?

In medieval times, the Church suggested a rational alternative to *samsara*, though the view that it mistakenly propagated went far beyond any stance which had biblical support. The view was taken that, immediately following death, the soul went to a place of cleansing - called *purgatory*. Though they accepted that Christ's redeeming and atoning death paid for all of his followers' sins - once the sins were confessed and repented - they believed that good deeds, or good *karma*, were required as proof that the sinner was truly sorry for what he had done. With no scriptural support, the medieval Church claimed that the good deeds that were not done in life would have to be performed over millions of drab years in this limbo-like purgatory. In this stygian place, eons might pass during which the soul would pay for all its misdeeds performed in life.

This *purgatory* was the catholic equivalent of endless lives lived to pay off the karmic debt.

People in medieval Europe were not, in general, afraid of Hell. They believed that they were assured of a place in God's Heaven as long as they sincerely repented of their wrong-doing, accepted the teaching that Christ had died to make it possible for them to be forgiven, and lived their lives in a Christ-like manner. It was only the terrifying thought of purgatory that alarmed and intimidated them, with its millions of years of punishment before they could taste the joys of Heaven.

Not content with devising dodgy dogma, the medieval theologians also dreamed up a remedy. The medieval Church *invented* a convenient doctrine of the treasury of grace. This was said to be a bank in which were deposited all the good works of the holy men, and all believers. People who fell short of a good life, and had not done enough good deeds, could draw on this treasury as though it were a bank account. (The idea is similar to the concept in *Mahayana Buddhism* - from where it may have been stolen - which permits the good deeds of Buddhist 'saints' or *bodishatvas*, to be transferred to others.) A paper *indulgence* acted like a cheque. It was a ticket directly to Heaven which could be bought for cash from the priests, or earned by pilgrimages or by worshipping the bones of Christian holy men. What a travesty!

The psychological crux in medieval catholisism and post-Vedic Hinduism is strikingly similar. In both instances, these doctrines were developed by philosophers and priests whose reasoning was biased by personal prejudice. In both cases, you don't need to be a psychologist to spot that priests Hindu and Catholic alike had excellent personal reasons for stepping beyond their scriptures in order to make of themselves valued intercessors - with a role to play in reducing the effect of the karmic debt (or weight of sin) through ritual means, providing services for which the worried penitent would gladly *pay*. The priests and gurus clearly showed a bias within their reasoning, which may not have been totally unconnected with a desire to make money and to hang on to their jobs!

The Moral Argument

Still, many Hindus believe that: 'the universe is undergirded by the spirit of *Brahman*, and that all human creations crave for *moksha*, or release from earthly bonds in the merciless cycle of *samsara* caused by *karma* - meaning deeds or actions whose consequences have to be worked out in successive lives when they are reborn on earth after their present life', to put practical Hinduism in a nutshell. It is very difficult for the Asian mind to break away from this scenario, so deeply is it ingrained.

The moral argument for samsara as the 'great leveller' is so compelling and hard to refute that, had this book been written circa 1970 it would have taken a different route at this juncture because, at that time, both Ram and Mike accepted reincarnation as a fact of life (and death). Ram because he was a practising Hindu, and Mike because he was an early New Ager, disillusioned by ritual Christianity.

'Those whose conduct here has been good will quickly attain a good birth,' says the *Chandogya Upanishad*. 'But those whose conduct here has been evil will quickly attain an evil birth, the birth of a dog, or the birth of an outcaste.' It all sounds so just and fair.

Yet, this belief has several serious moral shortcomings. Firstly, it justifies failure to help the poor, the ill, the starving and the homeless. The outcaste and the underdog are in that state because it is their just reward of *karma* for nefarious deeds in past lives. Compassion and self-sacrifice are frowned upon because they simply delay the repayment of the bad *karma*. The *samsara* doctrine provides a good excuse for not doing your *dharma*! Consequently, the work of helping the poor in Calcutta is left to Christian missionaries like Mother Theresa:

> *'By blood and origin, I am all Albanian,*
> *My citizenship is Indian, I am a catholic nun,*
> *As to my calling, I belong to the whole world,*
> *As to my heart, I belong entirely to Jesus.'*

Secondly, the reincarnation concept defers the responsibility for dealing with social ills in the here and now. It gives no incentive for medicine or health care: why heal someone if their sickness is a punishment for a depraved deed in a previous existence? There's no need to rush if you're going to be around for another few million years...

Thirdly, *samsara* denies the uniqueness and value of each human life. Many Chinese people in particular consider it beneath human dignity to regard man as no more than an animal in clothing, on a par with plants and insects, so Hinduism has made little headway in China.

Then there are the practical problems:

i) There are disturbances in the world that cannot be paid back. Can a General who invades a country be repaid by *being* a country, and by being invaded himself? It's so impossible, the bizarre idea is totally demented!

ii) If the soul existed before the body, where did it live? and what was it doing there? If it didn't have any karma, how did it get born in the first place?

iii) Hindu belief is often inconsistent with itself, theologian Hans Kung believes. If there was an absolute beginning to the world, as Hindus believe, what previous *karma* can the first man have had to work out? Surely not *karma* from animal, vegetable or mineral existence; there is no sin in those spheres. God has not revealed himself there, runs Kung's argument, so there can be no transgression of God's will at those levels. As Mark Twain said, 'Man is the only animal that blushes; or needs to.'

Some have suggested that objective *proof* exists for the reality of reincarnation, but none of the cases put forward - usually involving people who claim vague memories of 'past lives' - have ever been substantiated. These "past lives" are usually the result of information acquired through reading which is then consciously forgotten, but available to the sub-conscious mind. Some, though, plausibly suggest some form of demonic activity.

Some occult books have suggested that there is a *vehicle of vitality* which connects the spirit body with the physical body during life. Upon death, this is said to come loose and drift away, carrying with it ingrained thought patterns and details of some earthly memories. Some believe that these are occasionally seen as ghosts. If these 'shells' which are said to lack sentience or life or their own, should accidentally connect with a living body, some think that memories might be conveyed across and be mistaken by the recipient as a past life that they themselves have lived, when it is actually a form of possession.

The Moral Crux

To the Hindu mind, reincarnation explains the inequalities and injustices which they say would otherwise be inexplicable. It is intended to introduce an element of justice into the divine equation; but there are alternative explanations. In Christianity, the inexplicable is made comprehensible by seeing *sin* as the major cause of injustice and inequality - with justice coming *through judgement after death*.

Reincarnation is a pernicious concept that is at odds with Judaism, Christianity and Islam alike. All three faiths teach that we live once only, then comes judgement, but no return to earth to keep living life after life until we get it right. From the standpoint of those three faiths then, the Hindu religious system *achieves* its aim of ending merciless the cycle of reincarnation; the trouble is that its adherents never *were* going to be trapped in a cycle of endless rebirth on the physical earth!

In its own terms though, Hinduism seems to disagree with the other faiths not only on the *samsara* issue but also on the greater matter of Man's eternal destiny.

Christ's followers are assured that they will go to be with Christ; and for a lover of Christ, that is ample assurance - no more needs to be said. A follower of Christ would no more challenge that fact than a son brought up in a loving home with kind and compassionate parents, would challenge the fact of his father's love.

Krishna's explanation in the Gita was 'follow God's true incarnation and you won't be reincarnated'. Carrying a heavy karmic debt, is like carrying any other form of debt. When do you decide to go bankrupt and admit that you can't possibly pay off what you owe - even if you have millions of years in which to do it? The long period of time only delays the inevitable failure.

For goodness sake, *Isvara* is waiting with a cheque to pay off your debts for you; forget your stubborn pride and take the gift that is freely offered!

Sari'N'Dowry

Allowing someone else to pay your debts for you is a revolutionary concept for many Asians, because it replaces sterile legalism with living grace.

The old concept has parallels with the tradition Asian matrimonial system, whereby a bride's family is usually expected to pay a sizable dowry to the groom's family before the marriage can go ahead. Often this legalistic requirement causes grave hardship to the bride's family as they struggle to provide fortunes as an inducement for the groom's family to accept the bride.

The marriage may be entered into more because of the financial rewards than because the young couple are compatable. Many suspicious 'kitchen deaths' take place in Asian homes where a new daughter-in-law is tragically burned to death in domestic 'accidents' which never seem to harm any other family members, and which conveniently leave the groom free to marry again - and for his murderous, money-grabbing family to receive another large dowry in the process!

In the west, such unequal marriage arrangements - which often sow seeds of resentment which can split families and cause misery to young brides whose family still owes part of the dowry - are gradually being superceded by so-called 'sari weddings' that are closer to the western pattern. Here, the groom's family show grace in asking - not for extravagant money and property settlements - but simply for the bride to be married to the groom *bringing nothing with her but the sari that she wears*.

In this situation, it is unknown for the girl's family actually to send the girl just with a sari - there are always other lavish gifts, too. But these generous gifts are given - not from any desperate need to please the groom's family, or from fear of social disgrace - but as *tokens of grace*, acts of unmerited favour bestowed as a way of saying 'thank you' to the groom's family that outrageous and extravagant presents have not been demanded.

A 'sari wedding' subverts the outmoded cynicism of the 'dowry wedding' where a family enters into a marriage for 'what it can get out of it'. The true gift, the one that is really worth having, is always the one given not from obligation but given freely from kindness and generosity.

So, when God bestows his grace upon a repentant sinner, he is like the groom's father saying to the bride's family, 'This marriage is a love match. I want the girl to be part of my family for her own inherent worth, and not for any worldly financial considerations. Come, I accept your daughter into my household just as she is; no dowry is required.'

Of course, the bride's father will send other gifts *as well* - what Asian family wouldn't? But the gifts will come not from fear, but out of love, with thanksgiving. Similarly, once God has accepted someone into his household as an esteemed family member - with no dowry required - most people want to give freely of their time and money as a thank offering. Freely we receive his grace, and freely we give our 'works' as love tokens to say 'thank you'.

Such 'works' are received by God, not as an obligation that is due to him, but in the same spirit of grace which inspired the giving. The person has been accepted into God's family as a 'sari bride', and doesn't need to be proved worthy by giving an exorbitant dowry. *Bhakti love replaces the need for any requirement of karma to be met, and samsara does not enter the picture at all. God himself has already paid the price of sin, or karma, so grace and mercy can now abound.*

'Speak and act as those who are going to be judged by the law that gives freedom, because judgement without mercy will be shown to anyone who has not been merciful,' says the Bible. Once God has paid for our sin, how can we then be merciless to others, insisting on receiving lavish dowries when God has not asked a large dowry of us to enter his kingdom and to become a member of his household? 'Mercy triumphs over justice!' (James 2:12,13)

No one need be afraid of *samsara* once he or she has accepted gracious God into their life, through faith, and allowed *bhakti* to replace the unspeakable burden of *karma*. Accepting God in this way is like marrying into his family and, like all weddings, it should be a time of great celebration and rejoicing!

'From the unreal lead me to the real.
From darkness lead me to the light.
From death lead me to immortality.'
- Brihadaranyaka Upanishad (I.iii.28)

MOKSHA: *How can I be truly liberated?*

'Necessity is the mother of invention', runs an old British proverb. Asians in Britain have never been slow to improvise new ways of doing things, or to invent things that improve the old ways of living. There are some 1,500,000 Asians now in the British Isles, and perhaps the majority are Hindus. Some old churches have become new homes for the *bhakti* gods - Rama and Krishna - who may not be new gods, but it's certainly new for them to be worshipped in preference to Vishnu, Siva and Ganesha who remain the most popular back in India.

Syncretism has helped Asians to adapt. Hinduism is a human phenomena of immense magnitude; Europeans use analytical methodology while the Indian prefers synthesis. Temple rituals are even performed by women in the west - usually by a priest's wife, as a pragmatic solution if the priest is busy elsewhere. *Havan*, offering fire to the god, is celebrated in families, along with readings from the *Gita* and the *Ramayana*. *Arti*, the light ceremony, remains very popular in Britain. But all are popular as 'duties to be done', rather than as ceremonies whose meaning is clearly understood and endorsed by the participants. Significance can only be attached to actions that are truly 'meaningful' to those who participate in them; actions whose meaning is not perceived can signify nothing at all.

'The Hindu community in Britain provides concrete examples of the liveliness and dynamism of Hinduism,' argues Mercer in *Hinduism*. 'This is expressed partly through reform and adaptation to the new situations in the west, but it also has many features of what one might call a "re-traditionalism" because certain customs are more emphasised here than in India in order to give the relatively small communities stronger coherence.'

Yet it is the repetitive actions and not the meaning behind them that is cohering communities. The motions are gone through, but they have no real connotation, other than as something the Asian community can do together. The 'traditional culture' that is 'maintained' is actually an artificial one that never really existed in South Asia, where *Havan* does *not* take place in homes and women do *not* act as priests. It is 'duplicated' much as a child copies its mother, doing 'pretend housework' in a pretend house; but it is in no sense 'real'.

Are these artificial 'traditions' really even part of the same religion practised in India? And is it even necessary that they should be so?

Would it not be desirable for western Hinduism to become totally integrated with Christianity in a way that would diminish cultural tension, and produce a true east-west synthesis? This could be something which is new, though based on the best of British and Asian cultures, without compromise, and not pretending to be other than a new formulation, a fresh approach.

Who *is* the personal god who is worshipped under the names of Krishna and Rama, when Krishna is recorded as saying in the *Gita* that all worship is really given to God, *Isvara*, regardless of the name under which he is worshipped? Perhaps it would be better, since neither Krishna nor Rama are historical people, to worship the one true God under the name of their historical equivalent, Jesus Christ. A western name for Asians in the west.

If the name is unimportant to Hindus, but crucial to Christians, let worship be given to the one true God as revealed to all the world in the person of Christ, argue his Asian followers. Let it be the beginnings of true integration, not simply at a cultural level, but at a truly spiritual level.

There will doubtlessly be many older Asians who are horrified at this idea. Yet it could prove to be the salvation of Asian culture at a time when it is in danger of being completely swamped by western ideas and culture, sweeping across the world like a monsoon.

Devotional practices could be rescued from obsolescence, by imbuing them with new meaning. Certainly the practice of *arti* - of waving lamps or candles in adoration of a deity - is a particularly apt way of worshipping Christ, who claimed to be 'the light of the world'. The red thread worn by devout Hindus, and bestowed at the special ceremony of *jarnya* could become a joyful reminder of Christ's redeeming blood trickling down after his majestic self-sacrifice to atone for the sins of the world.

Western Moksha

If *samsara* is not a reality but only an old philosophical idea that has long since passed its 'sell-by date', what is the doctrine of *moksha*, or release, to mean to western Asians? Perhaps it is a release from all the ritual, whose origin and purpose have long since been lost in family antiquity, and a liberation into religious thought of a kind that has some relevance to normal life in the everyday world.

'Understanding' does not have a high priority in Hindu worship and religious practice. If conversation in the workplace comes around to talk of religion, the average Hindu will have exhausted his religious knowledge in a few sentences. Rituals are performed 'because it keeps the gods happy'; 'because it is our duty'; 'because we must'; 'because my dad told me to, and if he says so, it must be good.'

'It's done as a community or family, and there never seems to be enough time to ask the priest to explain anything. He always seems to be busy anyway; and I'm too busy trying to make a living,' apologises the industrious Asian. Life in India can be tranquil, but in the west so much more application and drive is needed to keep up with the hectic pace.

Western lifestyle and culture clash with Asian thought forms on the balmy sub-continent, just as they do in the west; but in the west there are no sinewy Asian roots to fall back upon. The Asian in the west is in grave danger of being crushed by the bolting juggernaut of western history and lifestyle on which he has hitched a ride without really knowing where it's heading. The only way to survive is to adapt.

In India, the administration, the schools and the hospitals were all established by westerners at a time when Christianity was still significant in western life. The values of modern India are therefore driven by Christian culture, in a concerted way. Those treasures won't be lost by connecting with the Church, instead, they will be returning to their fountainhead, to be transmuted and reborn. *Samsara* indeed!

Why try to combat the tensions of being Asian in a western country, when all the time you feel as though you're walking around with two brains in one head - the British brain likes denim jeans, and fish and chips; while the eastern brain likes eastern garments, and is partial to vegetable samosas...

Two Snapshots

She's lying in the casualty department of a busy western hospital. Her name isn't important; she's just one of thousands of western Asian girls for whom the conflicts of living in two worlds - being Asian at home and western outside - have proved too much. Perhaps she's your sister, or your niece.

Her parents would be mortified if they could see her now, being examined closely by a male doctor; but no one knows who her parents are, as she lies there, retching and gagging. She was brought in by ambulance a few minutes ago.

The nurses try to calm her as the nursing sister feeds a length of tubing down her gullet. She's been sick on her *salwar kamiz*, but that's the least of her worries as the nurse attaches a funnel to one end of the tube and commences pouring a pint or so of water into it, before lowering the tube so that the stomach contents syphon out into a bucket. *She's having her stomach pumped*.

Through a blur of tears, the girl - perhaps in her early twenties, but feeling more like a small and desperately insecure child - wonders why she could have been so stupid as to take a drug overdose in the first place.

She's one of the lucky ones; she was brought to hospital before the tablets she swallowed led to coma and death. Doubly lucky that she is not one of those whose metabolism is susceptible to the toxic effects of paracetemol in overdose. Stomach pumping would not have availed; within sixteen hours, the tablets would have been absorbed by her body, leaving her beyond help and hope. Bleeding, terrible itching and jaundice would have accompanied her slow and painful death from liver failure.

It had seemed a good idea at the time; a neat way out of the family pressures to have an arranged marriage, to wear Asian clothing, to go to the *mandir* or the *gurdwara*. An escape from the family squabbling had cruelly beckoned. She trusted the priests who said she would come back for a new life - a second chance to get things right, without the cultural luggage. Now she had been given a second chance in life - when there would have been none in death.

Some have found a better way. Here's one example:

Sadhu Sundar Singh is not an invented name; he actually lived in

India, last century. A devout man who could find no way through the religious maze that was, then as now, strangling the Asian faith; denying their adherents a chance to be thrown a lifeline by which they could be pulled to the safety of a spiritual 'yoga' that stood up to intellectual rigour - and by which they could actually reach God.

Singh could find no peace anywhere within the gloomy labyrinth, and was like a rat seeking for the way out. He was a Sikh from birth, though it bequeathed him only pain and despair. In desperation, he prayed that God would reveal himself, for prayer is the hallmark of the man of faith. He resolved to kill himself if the prayer passed unanswered. After an hour and a half of entreaty, during which he was expecting to see Krishna or Buddha appear, a light seemed to appear in the corner of his room, he claimed. Standing in the light was a figure whom he perceived to be that of Jesus Christ.

'In all eternity I shall never forget his glorious face, nor the few words which he spoke. My heart was filled with inexpressible joy and peace, and my old life was changed. The old Sundar Singh died, and a new Sundar Singh, to serve the living Christ, was born.'

Of course, such phenomena is extremely rare, and we will later come to see that mystical experiences, though they *do* occur, are seldom essential as a catalyst for faith transformation. Christian theologian Hans Kung, accepts that mystical experience in different religions have elements of common ground, yet recognises that there are also conflicts and differences.

Singh had come to know true *moksha* - liberation from sluggish superstition and the unbearable straining to conform to culture. This is the kind of *moksha* needed by the suicidal girl who couldn't cope and tried to snuff out her own future. She thought she could be born again into a new life, when she needed to be re-born of the Spirit of God.

Liberated *From*

It is presumed by the ill-informed that salvation is an exclusively western idea; that people from the east need only the liberation of *moksha*, and not to be 'saved' from anything.

Yet there are a commonwealth of religious terms which express aspects of salvation within the Hindu framework. There is *tarana*, meaning 'causing or enabling to cross', an act which requires a saviour figure; *uddhara* is the act of raising up, and for Sankara 'upward' meant rebirth as a god, while Ramanuja understood it as release from the world. *Trana* signifies protection and shelter, or rescue from the phenomenal existence in maya. *Raksa*, too, means protection.

The two words most commonly employed to mean salvation, though, are *moksha* and *mukti*. Both words have the same root, muc-, meaning 'to liberate or deliver'. *Sreyas* implies liberation to a better place or condition. In *bhakti* literature, we meet with expressions like 'reaching the feet of God' the mystical goal to which liberation aspires.

There are many other words meaning salvation, but these are perhaps the most common. Hindu faith has been unduly criticised by Jews, Christians and Muslims alike for its failure to fully acknowledge the existence of sin defined as 'disobeying God'. 'Hinduism most often places the ills of the world on the individuals *ignorance of his own supposed divinity*, rather than on the individual's own shortcomings and wrongdoings,' runs the argument of those other faiths. It's an ill-informed objection, though, because the concept of *sin* - in a very Judaeo-Christian form - is clearly found amongst most Hindus, and it is really only the *jnana* tradition that emphasises people's inate *ignorance* of their own conjectured condition.

In Islam, heaven and hell are firm tenets of faith. 'Allah is merciful' is forever on a Muslims lips, but there is no assurance in Islam that he will be! It is difficult for the average Muslim to conceive of heaven as intimate fellowship with God, though the mystic Sufis accept that it is true. Good deeds outweighing bad deeds are the only way a Muslim believes that hell can be escaped.

The western mind easily makes mistakes in trying to grapple with eastern faiths. Conversely, western theological thought forms are often difficult to incarnate within Asian culture.

'I tell you the truth, whoever hears my words and believes him who sent me has eternal life and will not be condemned; he has crossed over from death to life. I tell you the truth, the time is coming and has now come when the dead will hear the voice of the Son of God and those who hear will live. For as the Father has life in himself, so he has granted the Son to have life in himself. And he has given him authority to judge because he is the Son of Man.' *(John 5:24-27)*

In Asian clothing this could be expressed as: '*nirguna braman* has consciousness as an attribute, sustains every thought and action and surely cannot forget anything, but *Saguna Brahman* is a personal God with the ability to will himself to forget a transgression, once it has been confessed.' What a joy to face final judgement, say Christians, at the mercy of one who has the ability to will himself to forget people's sins!

Liberation *By*

From the *Gita*, salvation can be defined as 'participating in God's mode of existence'. It is only possible because of God coming down to earth with his whole essence. An individual's unaided efforts will not suffice - salvation is a gift given by *Isvara*, through grace. God intervenes personally through his incarnation to save souls from bondage; he attracts them, and instructs them, being ever active in the souls of his followers through his imminent presence. He is the father of the world, the friend of every created being, infinitely merciful to all who turn to him. As the *Gita* has it, to his devotees he is like a father to a son, as a friend to his friend, as a lover to his beloved.

This Lord is Krishna, yet Krishna is not a figure of history, but of supremely mythological literature; unlike Christ, who was and is the living fulfillment of all that was offered and promised by the mythical story of Krishna.

To many Hindus, liberation means attaining to the freedom of immortal life in bliss. 'Because God is by definition eternal and unchanging, the soul also participates in God's mode of existence and activity without being identical to him, since God transcends the temporal and eternal as their overseer,' says Dhavamony. 'Love of God not only leads to salvation but constitutes the liberating state itself, for it is by love that one lives in union with God. But God's intervention as *avaitara* and grace are absolutly necessary for man to reach salvation, since by his own powers man is unable to do what is required for salvation, namely to be morally perfect, know God as he truly is, and to love him.'

Hindus and Christians alike can agree with this quotation, though Christ's followers would like to add a further corollary: 'Salvation comes by grace, through faith, *only* because of the magnificent self-sacrifice of God incarnate as an offering to atone for the sins that would otherwise still keep man irreconcilably separate from God.' Just as the ancient *brahmin* priests sought to redeem those on whose behalf they sacrificed, by pleading for the sacrifice to be accepted as a symbol of the offerer's own body which he does not deserve to keep, so Christ offered himself as a substitute to redeem his followers' own bodies.

The *Gita* began a theistic change of emphasis for *moksha*, away from the idea of some distant liberation to an immediate and direct relationship with God. From some abstract philosophical concepts which must have seemed like so much hocus-pocus to the common people, the *Gita* simplified the principal theistic strand to the equivalent of a simple love letter, a kiss and a hug: this was God saying, 'I Love You' in the most direct possible terms.

'By knowing the One God who envelopes the entire universe on all sides, man is released from all bondage.' (*Shvet Upanishad 5.13*) 'Knowing God' refers not to arcane spiritual knowledge, nor mere information gleaned from books, but *knowing him in the way that a child knows a parent.* 'The fire of knowledge reduces all *karma* to ashes.' (*Gita 4.37*)

St Paul affirmed that it is knowing a *person*, and not mere academic knowledge which makes the life-transforming difference. Speaking of the faithful commitment he himself made to God in Christ: 'I know whom I have believed and am convinced that he is able to guard what I have entrusted to him.' (*2 Timothy 1:12*)

Liberated *For*

Klaus Klostermaier (*Mythologies and Philosophies of Salvation in the Theistic Traditions of India*) insists that even the old Vedic concept of salvation is not restricted to freedom and bliss on earth, nor escape from the law of cause and effect, but includes immortality in an afterlife: 'Many hymns in the *Rig Veda* speak of heaven and the beyond.'

He illustrates from the Vedas that in the 'world of the fathers' the soul will again have a glorious body for 'a life of bliss, free from imperfections and bodily weaknesses'. The Vedic heaven is a place 'where Brahma reigns supreme, where there is eternal light.'

Around 500BC, the snooty upanishadic sages began to reject rituals as good only for those who wanted prosperity in a material heaven little different from the earth. They themselves set their sights higher - certainly higher than *samsara* - desiring the supreme illumination that *they* described as *moksha*: release from physical pleasures and the attainment of knowledge of God. Far from expecting to be reborn on earth, they even rejected any desire to live in a beautiful Heaven, desiring instead to 'be with God' and to